WellSpringEternal

Every day is a blessed gift. Every breath, exhale, heartbeat, and footstep is such a cherished, loving gift. Every drop of dew nestled on leaves, falling upon the flowers and grass, is so playfully loved, appreciated, and used by the greatest silent giver of all life, mother Gaia. Every head held high with lifes victories are but a glimmering speckle of new beginnings and the start of anothers journey, anothers end, anothers pain, anothers voice. Screaming, weeping, laughing, scoffing, gentle, boisterous, arrogant, cutting, mending, prudent, diligent, taking, giving, the choice is always yours. Every day spent alone in absolute silence is a gift. Every day spent with friends and family is a joyous gift. Every road, bridge, mountain, river, forest, frozen tundra and lush jungle we as one walk upon slowly in high regard, is such a gift. Every fire burning, scorching the ground while pushing the iron wheeled carriers of life, is a sacred honored gift. Every bite, morsel, drop, flavor and taste, placed in and upon your mouth is so sacred, and always should be brimming with only the energies of sun, growth, light, and life. Every word you speak, write, and which falls upon your ears, or the ears of another, holds great potential to instill an enduring appreciation for all beings to touch future generations leaving a lasting impact, while lighting the torch for others to bear.

Upon a mighty plain where by his sons, brothers, and fathers before him, yoked the beast tilled the land cleared away stones and plucked weeds, there lived a young boy ever so eager to do his part and make reap the yearly harvest to make full the bellies of his sister, mother and dogs as they toiled to stay warm through the cold, dark, dreary months of the great mothers slumber.

Every season the rains came, the animals fertilized the ground, and pollen grain spread across the plains by the buzzing bees and winding winds. Every season as the reaping scythe cycled upon the land, father placed bags upon oxen walking through the fields shaking, coercing, and freeing the seeds from grains, trees, roots, and pitted fruits. Every year the young boy knew of this day when his father would before him open the large wooden chest in which the burlap bags of seeds were kept. Sternly as his fathers father had spoken unto him, and with the same solemn look of important intensity, father uttered: Boy, the great mother holds, as she gives life form over many days, nights, and moon cycles. We need only to gather, keep dry, and honor the core essential kernel of creation stored lovingly, free of all light, dampness, and pollen. We protect her bounty. His hand picked up the seeds, and as they flowed through his fingers he checked each one, turning, nurturing, aerating, honoring, bellowing and loving. In that love was his commitment to the great seed which had been sown upon the fertile ground by his fathers hand, and his grandfathers hand.

Looking down upon his son, he placed one hand upon his shoulder, and one seed in the palm of his hand, saying thus: This seed, fed by the loving warmth of your hand, has written within it the cycles of life, death, and birth. One day I will return back unto the land taking in my last breath, joining with the earth, air, water, and fire, as the great hand of time comes to harvest all life. As we harvest life from the ground, we return. But as this seed reminds us, the core truth of springs return and the warmth of summer is always followed by the change of fall and winters cold relent. This seed of life liveth in you and within me. Though I will one day be not of the flesh, I will always be part of you, part of the land, and one with the ground, wind, and rain. Be not sad for me as my skin is old and burnt, my back weary from the daily toils, and my hands ache from all the years of picking, pruning, planting, and plowing thus.

  The young boy with tears in his eyes at the thought of his fathers departure, held the seed tightly in his hand, close to his heart. Content with his sons knowing, father took out the burlap bags, and quietly went about lovingly filling them with seed.

Closing the heavy door behind them, he went about plowing up the ground to make ready soil beds that lay moist, aerated, and fertile, from the great care given to let rest the fields after a prior years harvest. So full was the bountiful and plentiful harvest, that many in the city, and those needy, who only took from the land, not always giving back, grew accustomed to the excess seed and grain we gave out freely and joyfully so they may bind the bread, and ferment the fruit for wines. For jovial and carefree be the man sleeping through the warm day, to drink fool heartedly through the dark cold night. Sternly, father reminded the young boy of this deeper knowing, for man reaps what one sows. For the balance of night unto day, cycle unto seasons, giving and taking, should be honored followed and revered lest your essence and knowing rot and ferment, growing brittle, leaving lazy the body, eyes, and hands. The young boy had heard this story before. His father spoke very little, and yet to his finite amount of limited breaths he hung upon every word. So cherished were his fathers truths and wisdom. The boy held these words upon his mind and heart, and they brought him peace on cold nights when the fires warmth dwindled into late hours. Oil in the lamp burned low, sands of time passed through the flame, as seed fell through fathers old strong weathered hand.

Fathers was a shoulder upon which I grew tall, steady, and true. On occasion, father would stop the old yoked ox carrying the sacks of seeds, removing his tattered weathered woven hat, breathing in deeply, he looked out upon the land, onto the lakes below, into the clouds above, upon the snow covered cascading mountain peaks casting shade onto the lake, and to every beast that relied upon them for relief and sustenance from the fiery sun. At that moment, I felt fathers wisdom, as he seemed to be silently bellowing out in honor, respect, admiration, and contentedness for seed, moment, cycle, season. Honoring in appreciation the plentiful bounty which sprang forth from pristine melted snow flowing into the lake, evaporating into clouds that when growing grey and heavy, cried out the mothers life giving rains to soften the soil, giving cover and nutrition to the seed. The nutrients from the ground, waters from the sky, and warmth from the sun gave all things needed for the roots to take hold, as seeds sprouted, fed by the afternoon suns.

Father put back on the old grass woven hat, then looked over at me, nodding his head as if to assure me of all these things being true. Though he spoke no words at that moment, I felt he had just uttered a lifetime of knowing wisdom and elation. Father time took father back unto the ground on one cold winters night. Many years later, I felt him in the winds as I plowed the ground. As my son looked upon me I took off my fathers old tattered hat. Looking upon the lands, I felt my father, and his father, and the great fathers hand upon my weary back. It gave me strength just as it gave my father strength so many cycles and seasons before, and I found true peace.

How many steps must be take until you stop and see all around your life trust, calm, and patience. How many battles and desolations of sacred waters must be fought and won until you lay down all armaments. How many drunken fools will dance dizzied under created pulsing lights, chasing the visions, desires, and molten smells of wilted roses until famished, wearied and putrid do they return home to healing, loving, welcoming baths of nourishing light. How many sharpened blades and wasted breaths will spill the venom unto the childrens ears until I melt the blade and the iron in the blood. How many animal carcasses must be taken internal to strengthen the arm, when this same arm reaches out to take, misguide, and lead others astray. How many documents, papers, accords, agreements and wages will be signed into law until it is seen with eyes open that man made law is another stone laid into the heavy wall. How many mountains, oceans, jungles, rivers, deserts and valleys must your flag fly its symbol over for thine eyes to find rest. How many glorious, glistening, glamorous galleys must you attend until you see that path leads but unto the gallows. How can you find joy in the screams, sorrow, fear, starvation and suffering of children. How many pints of forgiveness shall I dole out, just to watch as you foolishly toss aside all cares and fall face first into a strangers bed, your family frantically, nervously, searching the wayside for you. How many carats should fall upon your wrists, ears, and fingers, shining the blinding refraction into the great eye that confuseth all, until you see the path which you chose to illumine is the road of blinded, set in stone by fools with split tongues, ears pierced fully. How many mothers must hear of their sweet childs demise by the hand of another who wanders lost, corrupted by the unseen hand of control, consumption, and carnage. How many crowns must be defended, and how many tiaras must be pranced, danced and slit open, until you see the rings of old man time lain treacherously over your head, onto your feet, and over your eyes.

How many He-Athens must do good works to gain entry into He-aven until you begin to lay down guidebooks, capstones, and corner stories that He-has lain upon your mind brow and He-art. How many times hath you truly had fulfillment by acquiring that which your eyes lusted for, and for which your loins and heart pandered and pondered for. How many chunks of earth and smacked round whitened eyes must you chase upon poisoned man made grass, all the while not listening to the birds chanting timeless truths upon your anger filled ears. How many plaques, labels, awards, embellishments, degrees, views, honors, indignations, and sovereignties, need be bestowed upon you, for another to look upon you with trust and esteem. How many rotary rotations as spokes in the wheel must you experience. Allow all into your stockpile of grain and wealth, just as I have allowed all the virtue and knowledge to be had from sharing the Cup of Life.

Emotion makes us vulnerable. Emotion draws us together. Emotion lets us feel who we are. Emotion drives the nurturing of creation. Emotion is the key to knowing the all. Emotion links the chain of our ancestors to the past, present, and future. Emotion is the serum that all new mothers sacrifice for life to perpetuate. Emotion is the last breath and closed eyes as our loved ones pass away. Emotion is the sacrifice made for the greater good. Emotion cannot be bought, traded, stolen, taken or controlled. Emotion humbles the proudest man. Emotions will lights the way through the darkest valley in the shadow of the soul. Emotion seats the loving loyal dog at the foot of its dead master for days on end without food or water. Emotion leads the Orca mother to prop up its lifeless calf for hours days and weeks. Emotions felt fully power all life on every timeline in every realm throughout all dimensions. Emotions drive in all directions. Emotion is a sacred gift from the great crafting creator. Emotion guides footsteps of those blind and pushes the walker of those elderly. Emotion pulls the one hundred year old man to follow his beloved wife unto death as the thought of life without her be unbearable. Emotion drives the mighty salmon upstream to a home they somehow just know is there. Emotion defies the prognosis of doctors. Emotion reminds us of how perilous and precious life is. Emotion forges the sweetest dreams and the worst of nightmares. Emotion drives the captain to go down with the ship. Emotion consumes the mind. Emotion pulls the trigger. Emotion allows forgiveness. Emotion glues the broken cherished family heirloom vase back together and hurts not the innocent child. Emotion calms the crying infant. Emotion watches the only son walk straight into battle with head held high. Emotion shatters the heart and pulls the heart back together. Emotion allows us to feel our fellow beings on the fabric of life. Emotion gives strength when there be none left. Emotions sing the sweetest songs to those with open ears and closed eyes. Emotions cause men to harbor grudges over many lifetimes. Emotion bound together in Unity restores the soul.

There exists a great wheel. In this round form, perpetual infinite divisions counterbalanced by trinity move formless, beheld by the five actions. Spokes of carnal carbon consumption represented by animals balanced in light and darkness, hold true the ethereal dual nature of stars as all becomes none when push lends to pull. The back is unto the front, as the below is to the above. The elliptic curvature forms the basis of experiencing time. To fill a void, one must be and know formless empty nothing first. We sleep and wake. We joy and sorrow. We float and sink. We know of the something represented in the consumption seasons arcing through resonance maturing thus entropy bound unto decay. What is earth if held not by the water. What is fire if not fed by the air. What is water if it has not a vessel. Time is bound, sewn, held, gained, lost, and divided in the helical concentric codex of the finite image of beingness. The orbit spins and the axis loops coherence adhering matter to perpetuate one mind in all, repeating thus seasonal cycles of beginning to end. In the beginning, there was nothing, and in the end still back unto nothing shall form be yet again formless as the spheres of creation sound the trumpet and string the harp, collapsing the great wheel and all its spokes as into one minute grain of sand it returneth unto my back. The beckoning bellows out loudly to those looking not to the stars and all its spritely specks, glistening upon the backdrop of my most cherished canvas, and you, my most prized, loved, missed, and defended drops, of shared agape love. You are the jewel in my crown. You are the great circle crowned by the twelve tribes dipped in the waters of infinite source. Be mindful, for a circle round but turns in the same direction and this gives light to all angels, angles, and structures. A circle is to a square as a triangle is to a straight line, it is all form, imagined and created. Seeing is to be knowing, as believing is to be giving. Many sounds, hums, tunes, words, vowels, and syllables have men created so that man can attempt to sound the voice of reason and explanation of fellow man and self. Know how your knowledge is known. Be what you already know right now. Say unto others words you wish said unto yourself. Time is the great temptress and she lives within upon and throughout the wheel, its spokes, and all the systems of knowing thought up imagined and pondered by those before you.

The rest and end of cycles carved by the seasons held in form are the one and only. If you push control and carnally consume you will only find more cycles of seeing your suffering repeat. If you see outside of the wheel, and cycle all degrees inward, you will find the opposite of stargazing mastery, and in the blink of a childs eye the truth of play will magnetize you away from duality, beyond all stars, and home will find you.

Outside of time and through out, there exists a great hall. Within this hall lay every great composition, completion, work of art, and mighty thought. The all sees it all, and this hand lay upon the shoulder and backs of every creator, crafter, maker, dictator, prophet, teacher, composer, conductor, cleric, and pupil. Knower of all things, maker of labels, craftsmen of every and all belief. Seer of night, watcher of day, to rest, labor, weep, to be joyous tender and sweet, to be profound yet simple, to live, love, die, resurrect, returning quietly to the highest peak and humid valley still untouched by man. In this place lay every discovery, scroll, teaching, and portrait of those tall and proud enough to speak truth when others remained nestled safely in the homes, pews, and synagogues. The power of choice driven by principle of free will are noble truths etched into every seashell, on every tree ring, in the gills of fish, upon the back of turtles, and within the eye of the iris, giving sight, drawing breath into the lungs of every man, woman and child. These truths are given freely, and without discord, horror, or injustice as harbored in hearts of those unable to forgive riddled with terrible insult of ancestors past, bearing the mark of thine brothers keeper unkempt, sullied, and dishonored.

The judges judge and the masters master. Keeper of great cycles, Setter of the sun, Shooter of distant Star, Crosser of uncrossable chasm, Knower of nothing, something, everyone, every thought, everywhere, and seer of all shame. All that listen to proud lisping boastful folly will find arrogance screaming proud, loud, crude cries of blackened hearts. In those hearts lives only payback, hurt, injury, and revenge. The great principles in the noble corridors of truth lend courage and calm to those weary, tired, hungry, and given up. Many stories, pictures, jewels, gods, and teachings are but a click or page turn away. Partake and drink of them to make full your cup of wisdom and understanding, yet be wary, for what good is wisdom if it makes full your heart with bitterness and rage. What good is a picture if it makes full your loins with lust and your mind with want.

What good is a deep thought of knowing if you look past and through the man suffering and in need directly before beside and behind you. Of what good is a party full of drunkards and talkers, if in the house beside sits a man comprehending the end of his life as he uninvited feels unwanted and unloved. Of what good is a friend if they burden your ears with gossip and take you to dark places where by the shade of shadows works its deceit and coercion. Of what good is it to chase throw and putt about a spherical object if it causes you with the vision of sight thru your round eyes to see not the truth. Many teachings are found fought and died for over that which sits and hangs in the great halls of knowledge. Many streams, pools, and bodies of water are available for you to drink from, bathe in, and take into your skin, to calm the inner thirst for understanding. The will and freedom of choice lay mightily in the garden for all to partake from.

The spheres of knowing and completion are thus: Patience, Compassion, Joy, Caring, Love, Forgiveness, Contentedness, Faith, Hope, Giving.

These are the winds you should find in your sail. These are the cups from which you should drink. These are the roads on which you should travel. These are the words you should speak to your friends, families, and enemies. These are the rights that will rewrite all the wrongs. These are the principalities of peace and the end of all suffering. These are the frowns and fearful tears converted to smiles and tears of joy.

Many men have written, thought, and spoken many words. How great will it be when unto a quiet mind and heart you fall and for the first time you know not only yourself, calm, full of love and life, but others, sitting being creating in calm full of love quietly fulfilling all others with the fullness and breathe of Life. This is the calmest music and greatest knowledge of all. Love of the all, Love of I am, Love of another, Love for your brother. In this place you will find your wellspring of life eternally bubbling forth, your cup runneth over. The gates are open, the path is walked, the steps a blazoned in celestial firmament. You need only to walk upright in Love and the knowing of compassion to enter thus from whence you came.

When upon the world you cast your gaze only flesh and the wanting of the world will you find. Be still, calm, and breathe in only that which feeds the spirit as a bubbling brook breathes life unto the valley floor. Know always the language of heart for it says to others hope, joy, compassion, Love, and good tidings to all. To be of heart with hearts beating together is to know your maker. Uplifted, united, encouraged, a flock moving in unison avoiding storms, threats, and predation. When you hear the cries of a mother with a child, embrace them and you will find me in that place. I choose what stands and that which burns for many are the wicked, clinging to past, lingering in the days and songs of old. The calamity and embankments sow seed and we shall reap that which we planted by action, spoken word, thought, and all time spent building house, bridge, bank, store, and jeweler, to fashion unto the I all that which is self serving and giving unto only I.

My Love for you, My patience for you, My oath to you, I will climb the highest mountain, brave the coldest night air, cross the vast stormy ocean, traverse the harsh sand swept desert. Hold the heavyweight of the entire world upon my shoulders. I have filled the oceans with tears of joy and happiness but also tears of sheering seething pain as you wander further away from the safety of pasture and protection of shepherd so soundly you sleep at night, the star sounds soothing humming purring dancing and singing the sweetest lullaby, drifting you unto the arms of an angel, nestled into slumber as you walk with saints, prophets, great mothers, and those with smiles so big they light up the cosmos.

When is enough, enough. When will you find the hearts key to unlock the gates of boundless plenty. When will I look upon your face, eager for knowing rest and calm. So many people with power, particles, pleasure, pain, pressure, fission, fusion, yet still upon your greatest test you fail. Men are people, women are people, children are people, people of all sizes, shapes, colors, creeds. All are my people. All are the same

in my eyes. To look upon all people with
the bountiful endless wellspring of love is to
know and walk with me beside still waters,
your soul restored as you restoreth the souls
of all weary, tired, homeless, downtrodden,
and withering upon the vine.

How quickly do you drink until
drunk, fool hearted fermented wining,
knowing not the particles that lay internal. I
tell the vines to be wined, grapes to grow,
and skies to rain. I bring the cooling winds
from the oceans deep. I calm the fires that
scorch the vines and make burning embers
of fortified stone buildings. I ease the winds
so the butterfly may rest and so bees buzzing
burst forth to spread next years bounty unto
the wind. I turn the tides, so the fish find
food, rest, and calm waters to just float and
be. I tie with heavy loving cords the
colossal rack upon the mooses head. I slow
the slumber of the mighty bear so restoration
is found through the cold moons and long
nights. I give might, strength and courage to
the salmon as boldly they march onwards,
somehow knowing exactly from whence
they themselves first spawned. I am the
snarling sharp teeth of wolves as together

they do rip and tear the carcass of any animal fallen from age of old. I give tremendous audacity courage and strength along with mighty feathers to the great penguins as they sit atop egg day after night after week after month patiently waiting for their beloveds to return. I give arching hollow bones and powerful gripping claws to the birds of prey as eagle eyes see from afar that which gives sustenance to its newly hatched young. I make full all mothers breast, so the richest milk finds its way to the growing hungry stomachs of all newborn life. I tie together the rings of every tree so grow high into skies they do, giving homes to birds, squirrels, and all lovely things which creep, crawl, dance, prance, and slither. I wrote poetry upon the slow moving turtles back so you can read and marvel at my handiwork. I give instant rise to the newborn gazelle its mother concerned not with prying hungry eyes. I gave the peacock its plume so majestically it raises its fodder for all to revel in its beauty. I made the seas salty and full of oxygen so the mighty seal may cool its wounds and rest after fending off others as it protects its offspring with might, gust, and vigor. I give

the sails wind and right the ebbing endless
rolling ocean so you may navigate the
mighty seven seas and sprinkle star dust
high above the Pleiades. I am every
wagging tale told by every dogs tail as they
eagerly loyally await your return home to
play as I, your maker friend protector creator
and nurturer, eagerly await your return home
so together we can paint the sunset, raise the
moon, and wish upon a shooting star for all
those lost and weary to return home as well.

Perched high on a vast windswept mountain range lived a mighty thick powerful untouched blue glacier. The winter snows over aeons of time had fallen and frozen, adding upon the ice sheet layers of time. Heavy, slow, pressing caring hands carving ridges peaks and valleys creating perfect nooks and hooks for creatures big and small to make haste for laying eggs. Creaking and groaning it forged a mighty crawl, its presence heard and seen many miles away. Days of melting and nights of freezing, many villages townships and cities far away from the frozen sheet of life, sky born from teardrops above, did garner pure water flowing in from above and bellowing up from the ground below as precious day light melted then dark night cooled, blowing nurturing flowing winds, sweeping thru the gorge and over the frozen valley floor calming, grounding, protecting those souls found safe and sound tucked into bed tightly, held close by the great life giving giants tremendous reach, might, depth, and power. Steadily the new snows came, building layer upon layer, forming gradually the great wall of ice. The snow caps clamored coursing downward as solar sun rays melted snow, cold nights refroze building layers, giving rise to the gigantic glacier. Continual cycles repeating, the sound of falling snow a welcoming sight to the mighty ice covered mountains, glimmering glaciers, and trickling waterways.

Time moves all. The giant slowly eeked and creaked its way down the valley floor moving huge boulders while carving massive swaths into the valley floor. Tremendous force, pressing pressure, repeating cycles of deep snowfall fed life, strength, and power, unto the blue true gorgeous giant. Many centuries passed and the blue crafter forged paths roads and etchings into the frozen tall fire rock mountains. Cracking crevasse within cratered crevices, the hidden life tucked caring into her folds as every year snows came forming yet another layer just as the tall mighty red giants formed another ring around last years ring. As the blue glaciers, red giants, and magma flowing mammoths cycle seasonally, the great mother forms slowly over many aeons. Molding, crafting, forming life in every fluidity. Flowing freely yet also freezing upon the tundra, tucked far away from solar suns and brightly

burning beginnings. All life in every form
needs time, cycles, rest, seasons. Arches in
corridors, bricks in pathways, thorns upon
rose, petals on vessel. Vast, slow moving,
layer upon layer, the blue giant grew while it
receded, beginning and ending, life and
death, coming and going, melting and
flowing. Pure, True, Sacred, locked away
far from prying eyes lived earths precious
secrets, frozen steadfast united with times
cords holding layers, crafting rings,
seashells upon the seafloor seeing simplicity
slow to a trickle moving at a cadence set by
the great mothers metronome.

Many flocked from all corners of the
entirety to drink in the sacred waters, to feel
cool tepid ice kissed winds upon the brow,
calming the fire of life. They came,
touched, brought fire, brought all forms of
thought riddled in want, naught, and all
manner of devious plot. Time passed and
the people frozen in wants fire, stoked kilns
of have nots and dark seeded plots in seats
of nefarious rot. Many men women and
children came bringing fire, litter, debris,
and all form of bitter contempt to the calm
moving ice covered steps. Eager for calm,
thirsty for truth, not willing to wait for

summers melt, they chipped away bit by piece at the layers of Love which reflected harsh rays and dissolved rage filled thought. The creations of man began leaning, leaking, loosening, leaving exposure to the delicate vital breezes cooling truths tucked tightly away in the hull of the great blue behemoth.

After days, months, years and decades passed, the fires and heat soared higher than the great condors. The giant melted much more than it froze, and the snow stopped snowing as once before. Breakage of gigantic chunks began calving off into the sea as her blue bounty pulsed, leaking, breaking, carving deep impressions. Blistering heat brought a most spectacular spectacle to behold as people in boats lingered from a distance cheering and screaming for the destructive show to continue.

They knew not the delicate sway formed by aeons of snow, cold, pressure, and time, as only in the moment of now did they want action boom and magnificent bloom, not willing to wait for the colds gentle gait. Yet the white bears, penguins, seals, and great orcas, cried out in waves of crashing cries and disbelief for they knew

the truth hidden and locked away in the
great ice vault. Tears of sorrow, disbelief at
the neglect as fiery formations formed
fractures and fissures even deeper yet. What
to do and what to say for our home is being
carried away by the harsh hateful dry hay
piled high on the blue giants cape. It is of
great sorrow and aching hurt that by your
indolent sway we watch as your self driving
desire burns, cuts, rips, and tears away at the
beautiful blue giants most delicate noble
face. The great storm is coming to carry
away all those that choose to stay in
vindictive, vile, violent fiery ways.

She has nothing to holster. She is
that which turns. She is a sleeping giant.
She lays a blanket of moss so tender and soft
for fawn to rest and for mushroom caps to
build domes throughout. She flourishes
when the rain falls. She holds safe in pink
rich warm waters periods of three life
cycles. She is, every heartbeat. She is the
etched, wind hardened bark wrapping the
trunk of every tree. She erupts in glorious
fashion belching out waves of molten new
life. She is our mother sister daughter
grandmother and maiden. She is precious,
as in her womb holds secrets untouched by
mans prying eyes. She is the keeper of
knowledge. She holds a truth refined divine
and precious. She forms, molds, cracks,
shapes, and moves to the pace set by the
spiders web as she weaves her spin spanning
the vast sea of time. She speaks in seasons
and waves. She moves mountains, carving
form, etching deep river valley meandering
passages, pools falling to places where
animals need not eyes to see. She is the
harness holding the parachute tightly to the
back keeping the thrill seeker buckled safely
into the darting train. She is the eyes in the
front, back, and side, sensing when little

ones stray from the den curious of the many smells, guarding against perilous pitfalls in the world. She makes music heard by every herd and flock, the song singing out in all directions, spinning the web of life in yet another cycle, another set of rings, another formation of clouds. Dusk sees her to bed and dawn awakens her, giving rise to leaves, trees, and all those buzzy bees. She asks for very little, only the time and uniformity needed to cycle as she perpetuates life with winters cold cruel freezing enrichment. She takes on all we give her. The hurt, trash, spit, vomit, burn sticks, corpse, her mantel sharpening, forming, and clearing it all. She is the very essence of nature, her poison cleverly disguised on the frogs back and behind the stinger. She is the refinement of patience, solid, flowing, burning, blowing, giving, taking. She nourishes, nurtures, suckles, meanders, flows, moving gently slowing to a crawl at times. She shares secrets to those with ears ready to listen. She sits upon her rocker waiting, wondering, wishing that her children will make it home safe, warmed by the hearth, bellies full, safe from harm. She pours out life, swollen, supple, and strong. She counts by cycles in aeons, centuries, days, hours, and minutes. She has many times sacrificed her life so that anothers may begin. She holds, presses, renews, and replenishes the seeds as they nestle into her rich mineral filled womb. She is a true survivor, looking for all attributes to continue the strength and posture of existence. She makes the trees sway wistfully bending this way and that as the highest of winds and fiercest of storms pummel land. She will be the last thing standing after every man plays out every game to no avail. She renews the sky, feeds the plain, and freezes frozen the windswept tundra. When she speaks it is very few words but profound and timeless in its origin. Held on her forest floors and in her jungles canopies are the keys to free the strands and cure every ailment. If to forage for leaves, caps, flowers, and herbs, these ailments you will never have. She gives fur and feather to those who require need of them. She gives gills and teeth to the swimmers and floaters of deep blue. She gives tails to all those in need of balance. She gives radar to those who navigate the night feasting upon the plentitude of many creeping, crawling, flying things. She gives great turn to the neck of those in need of turning them. She draws forth the worms after the rain falls for the birds to feed the fledgling hungry clicking chicks. She makes strong the jaws and beaks of scavengers as their job is most important indeed. She weaves the tale of creation onto every feather and within every eye pupil. She sees wisdom in the cold frozen caps that protect glorious glaciers, while most long for terra forming. She will cool herself if you cook and warm her too much. She has friends, fathers, fighters, and protectors that you cannot see with your blinded consuming darkened eyes of desolation. She has already won. She knows there is no fight to win. She has stashes of seeds from centuries ago with her old friends the squirrels that you do not know about and will never find. She grows weary of the manipulation and poison dumped upon her and into her mighty seas. She as yesterday remembers the giant dinosaurs roaming about foraging without a care in the world. She is confused watching you run in place when she has so many lovely places you could run to and through. She is the joy in a simple mans heart. She is the long sad bellow of an orca mother that lost her calf. She is the strength and courage of the polar bear to never give up when cold, starving, and alone. She is the loving petting and streaming tears of the little boy whose dog is dying, drawing final breaths. She is the cord that gives nutrients and life to the unborn child. She is the sorrow and agony of every mother walking away from the abortion clinic. She makes mistakes and does not look back to linger. She day after day allows us to continually poison her as her patience and love for us is tender, sweet, compassionate, and forgiving. She is furious, fun, and flirty all at the same time. She is the soft blanket and smell of grandmas house, so inviting and cherished. She feeds and holds true the boundary between life and death. She is the soaring majestic eagle carelessly gliding, perched high on the warm winds watching over all below as she is above. She wraps the cold, sick, and homeless, in a blanket of Love every night. She is the final match left to strike hope into the evening sky. She is our giver, holder, calmer, and forgiver. She will never betray, abandon, or unfriend us. She is the beginning and the end. She is our Earth Mother, and we will Love, Honor,

Protect, and Nurture her, until our last step
and final breathe to return yet unto her
again.

        Your fathers past insults wars
mistakes arrogance and injury need not be
repeated going forward. Your mothers woes
and calamities need not lead you astray. The
suffering of your forefathers need not be
perpetuated and left open to continue
bleeding precious blood. The past is not set
into the future unless to it you lay track upon
tracks. To honor your ancestors with
forgiveness is the sweetest song to their ears.
To forge a path of clarity is to see through
eyes uncovered. If you find the insult
unbearable look upon the mirror of time and
change the lens in which you behold
yourself. Let your fathers anger burn out in
him, carry it not in the torch with which you
look to burn down anothers village, as you
burn only your own. Let us forget and
forgive if doing so calms the winds of the
great mother. Lend unto yourself that which
is lent to you. Give to those who find not
forgiveness and you will live in peace,
harmony, and joy. The gates corridors and
hallways of your parents temptations, you

need not heed that call. Easy you will find a
path walked before. Walking the path
unknown, your heart striding true, gives zest
and firmament unto your stride. If always
looking upon the past through scopes,
mirrors, and books, how then will you see
the all which lives in the future. If the path
is laid out before you, bricks set heavily
with footprints of others, stop, take time, and
relish the possibility of pulling up that
firmly laid stone and setting it in yet another
direction.

How long will you linger, looking but not finding. How many times will you glance upon temptation following fools to certain death. How many storms floods bombs famines and injuries must you witness before unto me you do return. How many forms must I take until you see yourself in another. How many mighty creations must you strike down not knowing that you truly striketh down yourself. How many times a day doth the world remind you of that which you have not. How many books lay idle meaningless chatter upon your ears and soul caring not for your path home. How many steps back will you take after so many steps taken forward. How many of your doubts and confusions do you place upon the backs and hearts of those barely hanging on. How many suppers must you share with those that speak your name in vain. How many cracks and crevices must form until you look not at the flesh but lift your heart unto me. How many creations of fear, horror, and war, will you sup from and fashion until you realize that be the root cause of all disease and forgetfulness. How many painted brows elongated lashes and crippled toes must she bear until you say to her, how beautiful art thou, how loved and cherished art thou. How many games of deceit deception and treachery must you play to bring cold afflicted joy to your darkened heart. How much time do you spend chasing lamentations of knowing when you truly know very little. How many thick piles of earthen branches and dark oil must you heap upon yourself until ablaze in fire of wrath you become. How many insults must you inflame upon your lips to ensnare your brethren until you see that upon your back do you enslave yourself. How many bottles and books must you partake of until you find true peace and calm. How many blessings shall I send your way until you believe and look into your own heart for sweet knowing. How many shouting shouts and shooting shots are to be thrown, tossed, and fired, until you lay down all armaments and speak kindly unto all living things. How long am I to wait solemnly as you forget me. How many specks of sand do you see in anothers eye when you yourself are blinded by a sand storm. How mighty hath the red giants of century grown only to be struck down by ripping torn tears in one stroke. How happy

are you when witnessing another stumble
and fall. How many false narratives of
telling told tales will you look upon as you
ignore and dim the light within. How many
fools do you follow as foolishly you do
follow. How many pills must you take to
labor and toss about at night still finding
little rest. How weary hath you become
chasing that which you toss away so
carelessly. How many mistakes of men
before you will you repeat until those
lessons you do learn. How many names of
God will you forge and fashion until the one
true name you utter: your inner hearts voice.
How many children need to disappear until
you look upon the world as lost and
unfounded. How many steps alone have you
taken when striding together in grace and
play you could stay. How many advances
unto the unseen world will you make
looking for the maker and I am. How much
should I give until I take it all away. How
easily is your joy taken away being trampled
on by all those who take steal ensnare and
hurt for hurtings sake. How long will I walk
the gardens alone calling out and weeping
for your return. How many honest words
can you speak by saying nothing at all. How

many are led astray by the mystics pharisees and knowers of nothing of the times. How many paths are laid in front of you, only for you to turn away, lighting a path of your choosing. How many lights illumine the night leaving many rotting and rank as thru the entire day they do sleep. How many words does it take to say I love you. How many times will you pleasure yourself when you could be pleasing others. How many piles of bones must be fired upon until the final rains fall. How much truth have you spoken today. How many grateful gratitudes nestle in the halls of your mind. How many symbols must you carve mark and etch upon your already perfect form. How many lefts to turn until you find right your sails in a steady calm wind. How many eyes will you look too for solace and wisdom until your vision you do find. How many trials and tribulations shall you endure until you look unto the inner hearts calm to ready your souls return. How many of your friends comrades sisters brothers mothers fathers and daughters should I allow to perish until I return to reclaim that which you bicker strife and fight over constantly. How long should I wait to see the creations I love so much come home to find everlasting peace, calm, and eternal abounding truth.

She sits at the gates seeing, wanting, longing for the riches and wealth of men. Long perfumed hair, rosy cheeks, elevated foot upon fitted form. With lifted foot she glides about to be seen and noticed by all that long for her. She covers not those parts which entice and bring wanton fire to the loins of men. She flitters about adorned with jewels, gold, and pearls plucked from the hoards of those men eagerly racing to her door looking, longing, wanting, wishing for more. Her mother so proud of her daughter for all the fool hearty men she eagerly consumes and destroys. Every hair falling perfectly upon the face, every brush stroke so serene and gentle as it flows upon her grace. In her home many mirrors you will find. Her love requires gas, a tall mast, and constant clim clamor as upon the great seas she sails longing to reach out unto the heavens for the bigger better star. Everything of this world she has but it is not enough, she thirsts to drink from the cup eternal, yet she knows only of that which lives external. Set upon her side those who serve, feed, and give her greetings of glorifying great song. Praise unto me, I am to be worshipped, she crieth out. Her child within screaming out for the father and mother she so desperately despises. Great is her pain. Of her many sorrows she runneth from. How can she giveth to others when want is all she knows. So many anchors knots and bows. So pretty in the concrete city is all she knows. Why read to learn and grow when to sit back leisurely learning of treachery and drugged out bliss is of all she wants to embellish and show.

       To whom does your bell toll. To whom does your praise light and love go. Shine so bright when the lust for her nightlife does your bell toll. She barketh out orders to those whose job it is to serve her every wantonness whim and folly.

The universe so vast and astounding to the eye of the beholder is but the tiniest grain of sand among endless vast beaches of the eternal creator. Looking upon the holly stars and marvel the wicked do. But her time has come. That grain of sand I will shake. That clever place you seek to hide your wealth and ill gotten health will be replaced with humility sadness and grace, pining with tear stained face, ever hoping that you return unto grace, flooding back to the place you began. So quick to frolic in dance under the moonlight, sacred naked bodies on display. Cutting, adding, taking away, pulling tight the loose skin, filling the lost feelings with great tyrants new beginnings. All those seeking the gates of Rome will forever find their feet will roam. All roads to Rome fuel drunken lust filled parties of one. To the great five pointed roads, you flee with great reprieve. Red and marooned upon the blood soaked isle on which you hide, fool heartily denouncing the great maker as you feedeth the hand of the great taker. Pity her do I, long standing is my sorrow and tears for her, as I harbor regret for my continued longing to bleed forth from my wound the arrogance and destruction upon which the youth are led astray. Seek her beauty not. Lust for her gold not. Look upon her not, for her day is coming and my vengeance flails out. By my hand, the stars will divide and consume in showers of fire and wave larger than any seen before. Consuming those which cut, divide, uncover, and make wither their fellow sister and brother. Recovered you will be. Restored all will be. Reclaim from the depths I will.   Renounced from my gates for time Infinite they shall, until unto me they return, hungry, tired, weary. Humbled she will be. Be still and know that I am.

Be wary of the internal physical fire of lust as it will lead you astray. Be wary of the woman that wants of all yet gives little to her husband, children, church, and community. Be wary of the eye and all it beholds. Be wary of the corners four as it closes you in as behind. Be ever wary of all those harboring anger harshness and maleficent contempt as they long only for War and Strife. Be wary of the folded cloth keeper of cups as corruption oozeth throughout. Be wary of any and all pointing this way and that as they see a way yet know not the path which they walk. Be wary of those highly learned by books of past men for they know very little as they claim to know it all. Be wary of any device that flasheth unto you distractions of the days chaos and grief. Be wary of the tongue for held in it is the power to build great walls and to cause stumble perishing rubble of the same. Be wary of harsh critical judgment as walketh not have you in those shoes. Be wary of the idolaters fornicators and governors of the day as quickly you will find yourself buried with them in piles of shame. Be wary of those you see as homeless decrepit and lost for Angels surely testing you are they. Be wary of her sprinkled in scent and perfumed heavily as her needs will always outweigh the needs of others. Be wary of those men who square the pocket folds and tie among the necks as your name means but nothing to them. Be wary of the minds thoughts as quickly do they gain weight and drop anchors on unsuspecting toes. Be wary of that which you consume when you know not the farmer or vine keeper. Be wary of those who bear false grievance to the brother mother and sister, they speak idle claims causing stumble and blockage. Be wary of those longing for the great end to come hence, as began they have not. Be wary of any that cover the eyes for truly they hide what lives in the heart. Be wary of those trained to listen to your words then utter them back as into your mind they wish to make haste. Be wary of those most active during the darkness of night as surely, they hide the true intention. Be wary of those which look to lead you deep underground away from the light as blinded by day, are they. Be wary of confusing, long spoken prose as the mind is easily swayed by many words. Be wary of judicial happenings as men have always looked upon others to be hung by a jury of peers. Be wary of your flamboyant neighbors wife for she cares only about your looks and desire for her. Be wary of all that you want for it takes away from that which you already have. Be wary of the Sun Moon and Stars as within them the true nature of I am will not be found. Be wary of those who say much but listen very little. Be wary of waters flowing down the creek stream river and estuary when you know not what lives dumps and bathes upstream. Be wary of those searching for meaning as they verily know labor under those mean to them. Be wary of the landscape painted before your eyes as you be the one with brush and paint. Be with all others inflow as the rain falls over all the lands. Be noble humble upright studious and courageous on all paths you choose to walk.

Why follow another when you already are found. Why be born again risen and rise when you are already alive and awake. Why search, ponder the wonder, and perceive words writings and teachings of others, when in your heard of hearts it all exists to be seen felt loved learned and lent unto others. Why drink the blood and eat the body when you see not from which source it did arise. Why kneel and humble yourself before anything other than yourself if in the image of I am you are, have been, and will always be. Why dye the eggs and stain the glass unless the blood you wish to keep flowing. Why get high, jump high, and pray to the most high, if these put you out of touch and just out of reach. Why anoint with oil and make yourself most flammable. Why allow the eye and eyes to wander when the eye of the heart hears only truth. Why constantly chase the almighty when you are the grace love and totality of the All. Why look up when your feet are planted firmly down. Why wag the lips and slip the tongue to rebuke when you can lovingly, patiently and gently, warm the heart and quiet the mind with aqua blue indigo flames of agape love streaming forth as one moving

powerful river of created life. Why count
the nodes gaps stars distance and projections
if you find yet more confusion of thought
and distraction of vision. Why gild in gold
and enshrine the shroud or savor the saviors
thorns and nails if it was spoken and
finished so long ago. Why not sell the
belongings and give it all to the hurt sick
and needful others. Is that not what he
would have done himself. Why lay crete
and feet upon the great mothers back then
listen not to her playful glee and deep
sorrow. Why sing a song, repeat a prayer,
recite a hymn, if it has all been said done
and played out time and time again
perpetuating grooves and rings that deepen
etch and seer the message to flow in only
one direction. Why choose one path and
follow one message when you can be
flowing, seeing, knowing, going
everywhere, nowhere, and all places, as it all
is all just reflections of the all. Why
constantly carve ornate visions into stone
and wood when so quickly the ground can
crack open, igniting fires, sowing waste to
mans handiwork in one short motion. Why
place the sepulcher and angular additions
upon signs unless you look to harvest,

control, and ravage with ornate bigotry as
you seek the highest good while behind
closed doors you partake in the lowest lows
hoarding all which is given to you freely
from want of grace, heaven, and blessing,
when it is given of a fearful hand. Why lay
the same seed upon the same ground when
nothing pierces that ground pounded down
and soaked with the feet and blood of war,
vanity, treachery, and broken promises.
Why lift up the great mother to edify and
ingratiate her when the world is full of great
women and mothers in need of kind words
and cheerful song. Why sing songs of praise
to look upon the reborn with rebuke when in
your eyes live many splinters from the cross
that was already carried, the burden already
borne, the suffering already forgiven. Why
listen and follow the drums and guns of war
when you can cover your ears and listen to
only your calm, precious, loving heartbeat.
Why be chaste pious and holy, when the
thoughts of your mind are riddled with lust,
want, and holes. Why command and
condemn with commandments set in stone
by those you never met and know not. Why
go upon blind Faith and believe in belief if it
sets you upon on a path which hurts, judges,

makes widows, and fatherless children.
Why perpetuate a line of musical chairs
when there is but you as the one and only
conductor. Why break, take, make, and
jubilate the cake when you know nothing of
the baker and from which field the grain
comes from. Why expose your dreary
dreadful dead thoughts upon a man in a box
when it is already forgiven and you one day
will be the one to judge and forgive but
yourself. Why live in the shadow of fear
when you can live a life of Light, Love, and
Eternal Grace with all your fellow sisters
and brothers on the great tapestry of truth.

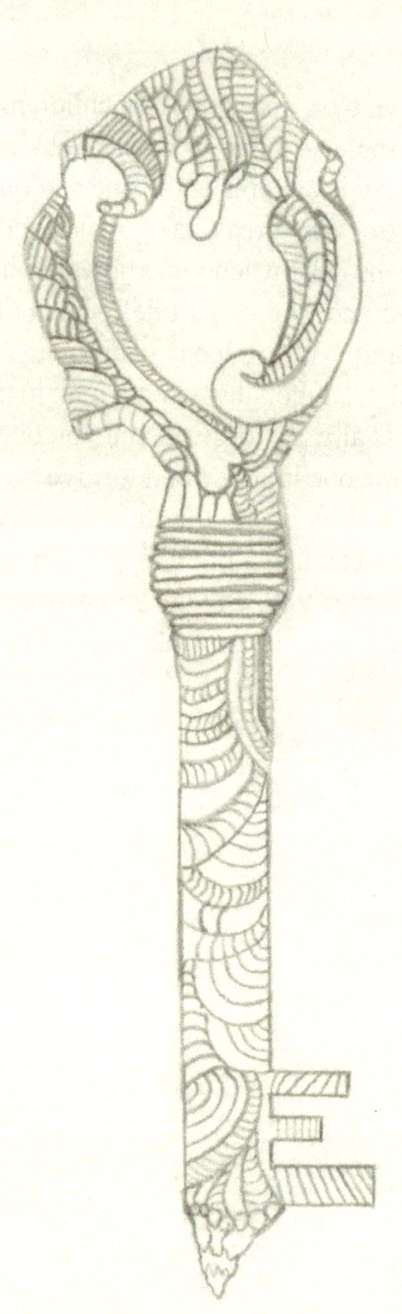

Up on high above the clouds lived a mighty mountain peak. Upon this peak nestled in a shallow cave lived the knowledge and cup of calm eternal life everlasting. This great peak was surrounded by ravenous dark creatures and creations all willing to scratch, claw, and climb the steep pass unto the cave to drink from the Eternal Well of Life. The rock face was smooth impenetrable stone forged of Iron and unchained by all cosmic creations. Upon the four corners of the rock face lived a compass, watch, shovel, and boots. Written upon the stone wall to be read by any looking to face the daunting task: These four and something more will steady your gait to open the gate for walking the narrow flow of time, so the climb made possible, your heart true and pure.

Men, Women, owners of much but wanting of much more, did spend resources to tame time, tearing triggering taking, consumed with fires flaming non caring. They spewed endless streams of knowing while forcing others to carry upon there backs the many tools books and riddled words of past so they too may drink the waters of endless knowing, seeking a truth wiser than any wisdom past, present, or future. Greatly tiring was the climb with many daunting perilous pitfalls to pass through if to ever lay eyes upon the riddle fours to effortlessly open the mighty stone steel enchanted door. So steeply high the mountain fraught with cracks crevices and creatures that many perished climbing the peak, trekking treacherous tracks left by others. Narrow was the small gap forged by the manmade path. Narrow the minds of those tiring endlessly for the cup of Immortality.

Day after week passed, the face growing with snow, ice, and the frustration creations which riddled the top and there in the bottom of the steely steep staunch steps leading to the great chasm, falling many fathoms into the deepest trench, only to open up to the closet of doom and gloom. The footsteps of many riddled the basin floor marking the start of the climb to which carved upon the opening at the beginnings end read: "To all seeking safe passage to know the great call of four, to step upon and through out the gates of the I ams doors, take heed of this decree: Come to in as out, travel inside and weary not without. In time the steps taken to guide directions needed to navigate fate".

Weary, Teary, and Dreary, the time spent stepping, struggling to lay eyes upon the great gate of wait. Many great scholarly men had poured over and pontificated amongst one another as to clues on the riddled plate so they too would never again face winters cold hungry stinging embrace. Wizards, Sorcerers, those flying on brooms of sticks, all conjured and potioned to change or make true cornered perfected pearly access to the honey laden path to access the cup holding eternal powerful wisdom so proudly they could hoist it high saying to be seen by all: Look at I, so smart and wise, I hath did that deemed undoable. I have walked that never walked before. See me for I am the victor. Yet still, no king wizard or knower of flying thing was able to pass through the seal, into the great hall, through the great fathoms, unto the divide of four. Yet tirelessly they tried leaving behind bottles, trash, animals used as sacrifice, and every other manner of used up not wanted tossed away trickery trash.

One day a young girl living a very humble life with her parents a single ox for

plowing, two chickens name faith and
believe, and one snake named I, did hear the
terrific tremendous tales of all those passing
through her village on the way to the
mountain tall. She listened to the men
named: Pride, Arrogance, Knower, Talker,
and Liar. She heard the stories and viewed
in their hearts only want, me, and self.
Many days and years went past, and more
people came while fewer returned feeling
distraught upset and bewildered, dead set on
the next time being the one when all shall be
known as finally the truth of forevermore
will be shone to all those who came seeking
knowledge, wisdom, and power.

     One day a group passing thru her
village tossed upon the ground a snarled
chunk of dried unwanted tense jerky,
hungrily her snake I darted down the pass
and consumed the unwanted morsel. One of
the men pulled out his blade to swiftly cut
off the snakes head yet she screamed, no not
I, that is my only friend. A kind man in the
caravan took pity on her seeing how little
she had but how strong of heart and back
was she from tirelessly toiling on her
families land to harvest just enough grains
and beans to last the winters frost. Saving

her snake I from certain death the kind man said go forth and ask your parents if carry, help, and pick up for us for many coins, could she. Her parents, feeble and old with age saw the coins as enough to last at least five winters and agreed so long as she did not attempt to climb the vast steep past. She rode with them and upon arrival witnessed tossed discarded keeping hoards of days gone and nights past.

Take heed around that tall pile of trash for many snakes lay claim and shelter upon, in, and ooo around it, be ever wary for many men have been bitten thrice left to wallow and wither upon the dust. She nodded her head in observance as the man set about lighting the torches and preparing glisten to gleam the glide upon the mountain so high. Out of the corner of her eye in the buried deep trash heap lay beaming a golden flash gleaming, and she felt her loving tender heart drawn to it, and it to her, yet it lay buried under mounds of terrible trash, treacherous ice, and covered in snake homes, but they knew not that she was good friends with her snake I, and spoke the whisper soft mellow language she learned running across the many snakes in the field on which she worked from sun up to sundown. She attended to her duties in the morning and night as the bold adventurous men toiled to climb the pass. Gathering firewood, collecting the fallen bottles of the nights drunken storytelling of tales past, she listened intently, and did all that was asked of her. During the day she began forging a path thru the mountain of debris recycling what was reusable making snake friends along the way that even began helping her clear the path as some could eat the garbage regurgitating it as shiny lovely jewels. She ever honest and true, gave the jewels to the men and so happy where they for many coins they could get to buy the shiny things worth buying. She cared only to unite her heart with the glistening gleam she was drawn towards deep in the rubble pile.

  After toiling for many days she made it to the farthest reach, digging tirelessly until she found the gleaming to be an intricately woven key beaming as part of a giant anaconda snakes tail named true heart. She humbly asked as to why she was drawn unto this key and the old gentle giant seeing in her calm, patience, love of others, and the great path she cleared so he could be free of the trash pile which surrounded him, did regurgitate the key and said to her thus: Many have come seeing, seeking, searching, trying and faltering. Many looking only for that which they seek, yet few including you do what is right, trusting that which your heart says. Take this key, read its inscription and your knowing will forever be exalted. Happy to finally be free, the old wise snake true heart slithered off unto the ravine to find friends, food, and a nice warm rock to rest under. She sat down amongst her new snake friends and they guarded her while she read the keys inscription. Upon your heart place this key thus and the rivers will flow unto you, the mountains will shrink from tall to small, lands will grow with the likes of every growing grown thing, flowers all around will bloom, sprouting, spreading, sharing with any place you lay your delicate grace. She flipped it over, and on the other side did awaken hidden words:

Tall is the grace found under the heart of the mountain. What is, is always that which you Love, so be Tender, Caring, and True, making haste to place key over heart, for the path is already walked, steps made crystal clear by those free of perilous thought.

Hidden from all who see with only eyes, she slowly hung the key over her head onto her heart, then suddenly all her love shined terrifically true bursting forth through the key of eternal heart Love trust, and a gentle flower filled fun easy glorious path shortened the tall mountain past. She exceedingly excited wanting but for only her family, one ox, two chickens, loving parents and snaked named I to have enough so they could play merrily, did walk directly past the riddles four, effortlessly crossing the perilous chasm shore, finding a rock face with an old embellished door, she spied a keyhole covered in years of dust debris and more. Excited, calm, and overflowing, she placed key in lock, opening secret back doorsteps glistening ornately with finely carved stories of those who journeyed before to restore the tall mountain of caring character to protect, nurture, and preserve, the wellspring of eternal life.

Pulling out key from lock, placing it over her true heart, she gently walked up the spire staircase etched in written scrolled scribing, covered in glimmering golden

living light shining. Slowly stepping
sacredly into the unknown so many had
attempted before she spotted a speckled
gleaming at the spires bend, as she looked
within the ending, witnessing in honor the
beginning, the past collapsed as eternal truth
emerged, for the cup is but a gift to be
shared by all. Gently reaching out, she
lovingly received the gilded glistening
glowing cup in one hand, with key placed in
the other. Suddenly, solar sapphire sounds
bloomed, booming brightly glistening
beginnings as ebbing flows dissipated the
entire mountain past and every fearful
thought born creepy creature crumbled,
shrinking, disappearing forever.

She stood before the proud great men
and screamed. Look I did it. Look, see,
Love is all you need. I love you. But the
men, confused angry and distraught, saw her
not, for they see with eyes of mind only, and
she walked past them knowing the loveliest
knowing of all:

The light of the heart is the key to
eternal forever. The path is long and hard
only if you make it so. Wisdom of forever is
true heart love.

There exist that which you believe, will, intend, see, create, and, consume. There exist only that which you create together eyes wide shut, the great eye of the heart open and flowing. It is as you make it. It shall be because you want it. What you are now is the culmination of your perpetual eternity, reformed, molded, and crafted upon the bed which you made to lay upon. There be but one maker, one creator and fashioned unto this same image you have this spark which alloweth the essence to pour forth creating in will unchecked and unscolded. There exists you among the many. There exists life and after death. There is beginning and ending. You author misery or you author joy. There exist in this plane of duality born of night and day choice among free will, given without want. Only the hope a parent carries in the calm caring heart, that all children will run from the wicked straight unto green pastures where the cup runneth over.

Amongst you, around you, in a
spectrum seen and unseen exist forces
beings and creatures alive and not that wish
to claim chain and bind you into onto and
within the shackles of time. In the ABC and
one two three, around yes and no, between
stay and go, lives the textures bumps nodes
patterns and programs whereby they lay
claim to humanity. Very cleverly over the
ages have they cajoled, corrupted, and
ensnared the shamans leaders and Kings
with fear, doubt, famine, fame, and
misfortune. To look upon the screams
hidden in the screens is to be transported
unto the false interpretation and trepidations
which hinder upward growth and choke the
base, looking to whither the stem to loosen
hull from seed. To look upon the creations
of digital data floating about the intricate
web woven with woes and wantonness lies
is to lay your head upon the malevolent light
laden upon your feet, eeking and leaching
into your fragile brain while slowly
ensnaring the essence of creation living in
the heart of all.

How easy it is to see what you want and do not have. How easy is it to tremble and shake when the cold sets upon you. How easy hath it become to lay your eyes unto that which frightens the mind and loosens the soul. How easy it cometh just to turn back and passeth. How easy is it to point the finger and placeth blame. How easy is it to pick up the sword of war and let loose words of judgment, confusion, and turmoil. How easily we do March to Spring into action at the slightest hint of blooming malice. How easily we snap, post, and share every bare inch and detail of our precious gift of life. How easy is it to look upon another and see different or strange. How easy is it to lay the sins of our fathers upon the backs of others. How easy is it to take without concern of consequence. How easy is it to knock on the door and ask of another yet slam our own gates, purses, wallets, and hearts, when upon our ear falls the same knock to our door. How easy it is to just cut, sew, cauterize, crack, and remove too remediate when a simple viewpoint internal of what goes in the body preventeth cureth and soothes it all. How easy it has become to feed the desires of flesh on every corner

and upon every screen. How easy it hath
become to care not and know not your
neighbor and fellow man. How great and
powerful the fear hatred and lust for all have
collectively become. How easy it is for the
mighty eagle to soar above others looking
ever higher giving no thought to those on the
ground below. How easy is it to toss
judgment and hide behind archetypes,
names, signatures and caricatures. How
easy it is to take counsel from a friend for
hire who lusts after coins and battle caring
not for your calm and melancholy. How
easy it is to have something to prove. How
easy it is to see the future, forget the past,
and live in the moment when they are but all
the same. How easy it is to blame the
aristocrats, wealthy, and leaders, when they
are the ones riddled with longstanding
worry, misery, and concern. How easy it is
to shoot words, weapons, and malice first
then ask questions later. How easy it is to
look upon the stars, blow a kiss, and long for
all your heart desires. How easy it is to
throw toss and consume that which was so
easily acquired. How easy it seems to skate
by while others have no feet to walk and no
eyes to see. How easy is it to steady that in

your aim to shoot an arrow, snuffing out a life which is the same substance in which you are made. How easy is it to win big than turn around and lose it all. How easy is it to cause your fellow man to stumble and fall. How easy it has become to pull the floor out from under those less fortunate. How easy is it to assume that light will flicker when the switch you do flick. How easy is it to order and eat, when know not of its origin or ingredients do you. How easy is it to pump the poison to go when the poison of many is hurting the lungs of all. How easy it is to pump upon the chest and pound upon the ground shouting: Me, myself, and I. How easy is it to lay alone, downtrodden, beaten down, broken, by yourself tears streaming, shaking for days on end. How easy is it to jump first and look later. How easy is it to force sleep with drugs when missing the sweetest first songs of the morning birds dew you. How easy is it to become lost in your thoughts and the thoughts of others. How easy is it to call forth the help of angels and mythical creatures when true help, love, and assistance, comes from within and from the hearts of your fellow sisters and brothers.

How easy is it to lend a helping hand and yet
you stroll about as if nothing and nobody
matters. How easy it is to look upon
anothers house to place blame, sharp words,
and drunken banter when in your own house
the souls are lost, untidy, confused, and
know not peace, prudence, and patience.
How easy it is to cause others to stumble
and fall when see not your own ditch do
you. How easy it is to charge, borrow, and
take that for gain stance or reputation, while
deeper into a hole you climb knowing not
the way out. How quickly is her innocence
lost never to be heard from again. How fast
does time fly by when narrowly the path
becomes fixed. How sweet is the sound of a
long lost friend. How perfectly the box
finds its four sides meeting. How perfect is
the roundness of every cell in all living
things. How great is thine own name. How
easy would it be to lay your burdens down
and walk past the shroud of shadows and
mental rains of time. How ready are you for
the end. How easily assumed your head will
rise from the pillow in the morning. How
easily do you embrace the pain and sorrow
of others in the world. How easy would it
be to live in joy, harmony, and trust. How

easy is it to take what is given to others. How easy has it become too sling sharp shady pointed shattered insults upon the hearts and souls of your fellow man. How great and mighty you have become with birds of metal prey and bombs of irradiant. How greatly you revel in delight at the long suffering of your fellow beings on the fabric of life. How great is my patience to watch it all unfold, weighing so heavily upon my heart. Do you know how easy it is for me to destroy it all with but one movement from the great conductors wand. Let your heart know Love, for I am coming soon.

As the all together united we are all mighty. There is no power but the true power of the all mighty, moving the seven seas, together, united, deep, rich with life, and part of a larger truth. I am the all, I see from the perspective of all. I am not my beliefs, labels, stigmas or angry hurting words until unto them I place my thoughts, hopes, prayers, and faith. We are what we speak, think, do, and put our creations spark unto. That which we cast a net upon drags us down to the dark trenches. Those with whom you take counsel and break bread do

plot, see, plan, and strategize the will of
men. How hath your will been drawn. How
have you seen the light in those even of
which you hate and harbor ill intent. How
will you know the all within if you focus
daily on all that which pulls and takes your
intention outwardly. You are a creator as I
have created you, made in thy image, great
is your heart yet simple is your mind. It is
better to wander about blind, cold, feet
weary of travel than to sit with men that
serve the hiss of asp and sting of viper.
They look to fool and separate you from
your wealth while smiling dutifully offering
all the world has to offer. Lay your life,
heart, earnings, and creations at feet of hope,
Love, and service. Lust not after the wealth
of men for it pulls screams and addicts an
edict, I set forth not. Great is the roar. Great
is the sovereignty of humility. Freedom is
free to all who long to express freedom to all
men, every woman, and all living creatures.
My staff guides those with ears internal.
The graceful and diligent faithful are
protected from the need for protection. Go
forth and open the gates. Allow the all to
embrace all. Lean not upon the past being
authentic courageous and of high character,

shining your light of truth unto the void of night where the wicked corrupt, fight, and destroy the light of life. When you are always home the lights are always on. When you stray to the honey mead scarlet lipped wine filled mistress your light dimeth. Awareness starts ends and begins in the eye of one as the seat on which the Kings throne sits, I thus allow. Tender and mighty is my love for it is our love to share. Ever present to every moment. Knowing where you have been and where you are going. The above and below are thus because I spoke it. What of the all in the know, concerned not with the winds and clicking hands of time. I grant long life and embed clarity to all that seek the knowing Eternal. The great fan of man bloweth small cracked shards of have not into the eyes and unto the hearts of man. Rinse from your eyes the shame. Remove her which looks to have you fight and war against others. The great mothers look to restore renew and reprise the keepers and protectors of life, so cherished, held for nine months, created in an act of Love. To honor and uplift our mothers is the highest quality. Look unto your elders and heed the voice of wisdom.

Many sounds lights projections and fallacies
are aimed unto the heart and mind of man as
is allowed. Every challenge a test to lend
the living loving light to those who wallow
in the weary rest of the wicked. It will never
be enough. It will grow taller and bigger.
How grand the mighty cities have become,
beckoning to the wealthy yet casting out
those who need most to pick bone and fat
from the trash you toss away, footloose and
fancy free. Those men and women you take
great strides to avoid, they are my soldiers,
angels, and groundskeepers in this wicked
place. But have faith, lend your mind and
ears to creation, not gamesmanship and fake
realism. How lost are they when to become
lost you do beg and plead. To be safe in
your steadfast calm inner voice is to know
salvation and to walk in truth now,
tomorrow, and for all time, steeped in the
riches of thine own heart.

There lay many upon you those which delight in the hurt, through deception, as a betrayal of all life. To be open receptive caring, to walk in the word of living light is to know true delight as men long to be served and worshipped by those less fortunate. Heavy our hearts remain as we silently send forth prayer. Steadfast we have been for as long as man have been men. So delighted in the winnings and profits of games and markets of bears that lost many have become. All you see looketh back to you. Every moment a constant mirror shining back that truth so you may examine your inner truth to better know the inner child and essence of all which brings youth, joy, peace, compassion, and love. What you attacheth to attaches unto you. That of which you speak is that of which you preach. Those you wish to stumble and fall, reflect steps from which you have fallen. How knoweth love in your heart when your heart you search not. The minds of men so very clever at conjuring, creating, addicting, attaching and devising clever devices so they may forget their hurts, sorrows, and pains. What is a thorn in your ear but a thorn you placed thus and unto another. The

light of the all mighty one will never blind
you, leave you in disarray, or have you
longing for more. So many false idols,
prophets, and those which scream out unto
themselves: Glory, glory, sing to lift up the
glory. But what of the cold man that hath
not the means to make haste to the temple.
What of the mother overwhelmed with
children many and resources not. What of
the diseased, addicted, desolate, and
desperate in your country and abroad. To
them should go the glory, to them we sit in
Grace. To be uplifting to those without is to
sit in the kingdom of kings and Holy of
Holies. So many chances beset unto before
and around you to lift edify and renew your
fellow men and sisters. The temptation is
rampant, there are few which cover up that
which leads mens eyes astray. How then
will your brother know God truth light and
conviction if all around he sees constant
reminders of want passion lust greed and
flesh. Tis better that you lay down all which
look to draw you from passing the gates
unto the spheres into the arms of all. Look,
Learn, Listen, Love, and the doves branch
will find its way back to you. Have you
given any credence to how hard it is and has

been for the all to watch as the loathing,
waste, and rivalry misplaces the tender heart
of man. Daily do we weep upon bended
knee. Daily do we send our shepherds,
scribes, and prophets, to deliver that which
will quench the fire of I. We move as you.
We answer every call. We are our fathers
keepers and mothers extra hands as tirelessly
she sacrifices part of herself for life to
continue. This is but a small drop compared
to the eternal stream of love which waiteth
for you. One drop of rain. One grape. One
grain of sand. One lost fawn in the dark of
night. One tree in the wide open vast desert.
One love. One light. One us. One you.
Together we are one and we run away from
temptation and suffering. Why hurt when
you can heal. Why hate when you can
Love. Why Look out when you can Look
in. Why deceive when you can receive.
Why be drunken of wine when you can
partake of the wisdom given in the great
cup. The trials will be many. The hardships
all around. The end is but the beginning.
Look to find the Love and patience among
the hurt and sorrow and you will know again
all those you miss and Love so dearly,
walking among them yet again along with

every lion, lamb, all sons of man as we walk together plotting our own course, building our own faith, restoring our souls, together we rise or together we fall. The tears will stream. The streams will dry up. The grass will wither, and it will matter not for we have risen, reborn, refreshed without hurt or insult ordained with compassion, embellished with forgiveness burdened only by those who chose the I. I am all as we are one.

Oh how much fun to fool trick and prank. What is real, what is not, who cares for it all matters not. Unto all would we say only a fool would use such a manifestation tool to speak the truth not. Devious dealing and misguided plots on any day may leave you as a lobster in a boiling pot. Truth is always the truth, and truth feeds the wellspring with Love, Life, Laughter, and leaveth none in the path of perilous disaster. If we for a second wander while frown and looked down on by so many, then take a look at what you soweth. Drunkenness, cheating, mouth and fingers running and tweeting, eating all that once had a face, spreading lies gossip treachery and deceit to gain the ear and audience of those that occupy a senate seat. The sky is falling, the mall is closing, the wolfs on streets bet on shoes you only need if you walketh on cold sharp man made streets. I am just pulling your chain, it is all just in jest, but to some that do not get the jokes or your fodder, the truth kids we will call them, they are left in dusty dismay and confusion because normal it is not, to deceive lie and plot. Remember the boy that cried out wolf, wolf, for when real danger is afoot and deviations look to tear out the life root, maybe then with your heart mouth and brain will not you shoot yourself in the foot. The path of distress deceit and falsehoods is a path unto the dark shadows and into the masters devious snare if you listen to your ego which chirpeth at night as the cricket. Be wary, alone in your truth and solidarity for the infinite roar of RA cometh and every cricket will be given a ticket to paradise not just lonely wandering around a clock within stay go and stop. Swaying bending twisting and listening until learn you shall that truth is home, and words, they do matter. Play not pranks and give utmost thanks for all you have and all you are. Maybe take a walk, smell the roses

of life with your brothers and sisters. Labor
not to honk beep and burn, tossing toxic care
unto the wind. The innocent girl in that
third grade class whose heart you shattered
with your vicious love prank, for her we
give haste, and it is why yet again we are
there in a flash to sprinkle agape love into
the fools drunkard liars glass. Shield of
truth. Love eternal. Love every day.

We will not be fooled. We will not be chained unto fear. We will not be fettered. We will embrace our tears. We will not look back to see the way forward. We shall not be pulled into the great dark abyss of deceit and unknowing. We are fragile and vulnerable and that makes us strong. We love even if we are hated. We will never fear ourselves. We will bring the bridge of life and tower of living eternal light to ourselves. We spend more time praying than complaining. We turn the other cheek. We swim in the waters we warm or cool. We are grateful for our wounds and scars and pass them on do we not. We are the foundation of truth built on solid rock. We are not pulled from grace and compassion with clever mirroring. We are ever present and aware of the great hands of time in honoring the call back to earth within its natural cycle looking not to extend unnaturally the stay of lifes place in the skin, but unto that which awaits in the next as we heed the call of the great hall and the welcoming of new friends and old. We are mindful of all forms of existence as life vibrates and flows in many forms. We are quick to drench the lips and soul with the waters untouched by grapes, for the spoils of mans wars are brought about by drunken lips and broken promises. We listen to unified hearts beating the drum for a great truth lay nestled in the breath of lungs feeding air with hope bringing joy to them all. We stand at the gates of unity marching to Mays showers planting to await November rains. We are guided by the bees watch and give to the pollen keepers knowing natures wisdom sits held in every petal given upright by roots firm hold. We know of our neighbors struggles and we band together as our neighbor watches and keeps the neighborhood. We are mindful as we swallow grace in every tear dropped in joy and sorrow. We have no gates for we have no foes only friends family and weary fawn. We the people of the earth unite to share the all with all living. We look upon the face of others and strive to see that which from whence we all sprang forth. We grow together. We share together. We care together. We all finish the path we walk for the need of placement is none. We relish the sharing and caring found in the group, tribe, together forever. We see in the wind rain and snow, allies friends equals. We honor and allow all life to flourish in every spectrum. We open the heart and give first to find the all giving back total fullness. We need no throne for a leader to sit upon high for we take little and give much. We carry the torch of our ancestors honoring every struggle and hardship endured. We do not see walls, boundaries, borders, countries, flags, institutions, dogma, and better then. We see but life, and the kindred soft love from a hug and warm embrace of our fellow brethren. We see how one raindrop comes together to form the vast open ocean. We have no need for hurting, battle, insult, proving, or savagery. We relish and hold the highest honor for the sweetness of emotion and the streaming tears of joy as one lost returns to the flock. We spring forth as rays of eternal light streaming steadfast storming deep into the cold parched dark night. We see only love. We see the value and joy found in love. We are Love. We take the form of that which we chose. We choose Love.

Holy is he that cares for his mother. Holy is he who be always there for his brother. Holy is the man that giveth his extra grain to the needy to feed the family. Holy are they who find time every day to sit look listen and pray. Holy is the man that feels all the grains of sand. Holy is he that stretches the hug unto loved one another feels. Holy is all which chase not the fruits of the flesh. Holy is the parent which takes time to listen and hear the childs call. Holy is he that works through the day and rest well thru the cold black night. Holy art thou which cares for and loves all the animals. Holy art thou which is a true friend to all. Holy art thou which heedeth the great quiet call. Holy is he that lights the torch of truth. Holy is he that walketh into the place of liars wolves and treachery without fear, wearing love. Holy art thou to which the worlds riches matter not. Holy art thou which sees in fellow friends, brother and comrade. Holy are those which face towards the darkest of dark nights until light they find. Holy is the father that forgiveth his sons trespasses and harsh words. Holy be the man that knows not the arrogance of the mirror. Holy be any with hand outstretched in Love. Holy be the truth found in quiet mind, stillness of heart, eyes firmly shut, all books closed. Holy the vessel filled and full of solidarity. Holy all beckoning out to truth in the still black night. Holy the bearer of torch very few look upon to see. Holy and wise be the man wearing the breastplate of Love. Holy all those quick to clean the vomit from the drunken stumbling mans shirt to then carry him home when he has not legs to walk. Holy the choice made for the good of all. Holy be the truth of time. Holy be all those willing to ask and reach out for help. Holy the souls in constant search of service to others. Holy the grand might of caring togetherness. Holy the Loving friend steadfast in silence catching every teardrop fallen from eyes of sorrow. Holy be the woman breathing encouraging words to all.

Accept forgiveness from any that ask for it. Accept only your inner voice when unto others you feel the heart stride bounding together. Accept little and give much. Accept only Love into your reality. Accept the gentle nurturing guidance of a trusted friend. Accept not the visions of death, hurt, anger, injury, and slaughter. Accept upon your table those foods most wholesome, hearty, and uplifting. Accept cautiously any standard belief label or stigma, most will lead you astray. Accept those in need of shelter, company, clothing, food, in giving you will certainly find inner peace covered with robes of service to others. Accept not the diagnosis of a cutting man as his pockets heavy with gold look to separate you from soul and coin. Accept and rebroadcast not the signals and stories of control, negativity, arrogance, pride, and avarice, for a lonely path these men and women find themselves upon. Accept only the road that you forge behind and ahead of yourself knowing in that moment your entirety is always affecting yesterday, today, and tomorrow. Accept not the shame put upon your family as you daily shine, work, and clean out yours, and your ancestors

closet. Accept the path you chose to walk
regardless of calamity as the greatest lessons
are those most difficult to catch. Accept
others and their shortcomings as I have
accepted yours. Accept invitations to places
of vibrant uplifting loving strongholds filled
with and ran by gentle, patient, caring
people. Accept not the invitation by family
friends and colleagues to places of
gambling, drunkenness, lewd nakedness,
and dark loud drug fueled palaces as they
look to lead you astray to take what little
you may have. Accept the ride quickly
making haste unto your home wherein your
wife husband children and family live and
play, there you make the calmest sweetest
music of life. Accept grace and be ready, for
truth easily navigates potential pitfalls the
likes of which vipers, asp, cobras, and
scorpions, lay in waiting for prey. Accept
the path you already walked and dwell not
on the past, for in past lay all your burden
and strife. Accept that you know very little
and find joy in that simplicity. Accept the
lesson and downfall of others for one day
that surely will be your lesson as well.
Accept the gentle soothing breeze as it lands
upon your face for it has truths to teach you

from the many flowers, trees, and leaves it passed through on its voyage to you. Accept the cool mist of the waterfalls thunderous roar, it will quiet your burdens and refresh the countenance. Accept every day as a gift knowing not if tomorrow you will rise again. Accept not the humor, banter, articulations, and jokes of dark men as cleverly they lust in hunger for endless power gold and fame for corrupted they are, runneth do they from grace as a hungry shark darts to bloodied waters. Accept only calm lighthearted fortification to your mind home body, and soul. Accept all that lives in the deepest darkest of waters for it is all a reflection of you and I am. Accept help when offered by cheerful delighted givers. Accept not the monies loaned by tax collectors banks and wealthy men, or cards of corporate, as in their pockets they wish to keep you always.

       Go where you have gone, see what you have seen, feel what you have felt. Embrace it all, every memory, every hurt, every insult. To be or to be not. To live or to live not. All you have, is all you have ever been, seen, touched, tasted, and experienced. Altitude starves the sensations.

How do you sense the variations of where you went, how you got there, and all the steps in between. The addict knows want. The mother knows tender caring. The father knows strength and protection. The liar knows deceit. The truth knoweth only of truth. Being what you see can lead unto thee the grace of grand reception. What you see is what you get and very often will lead to neglect. Far grander the reception when yet all are invited, none feeling left out, unstriped, unranked, or less than. Negativity stems its veiny black pearls of hindrance in the wallowing treachery and dreaded mistakes of mankind. How easy to forget when you see only forward the steps of all those before you. It is written and so it is. It is finished yet it has begun. It always leads to sorrow as Love leads to loss. Without loss how could loves truest lesson be learned. You guide your steps through, around, between, and within all knowledge of what you have seen, been, want, and are becoming. Deliverance from self love is clarity of self pain. Loathing sinister misguided and constrained the steps words thoughts and precise pre defined wantonness nature of man, sowing seeds of misfortune chaos and separation. To run in fear or stay and fight. Love or never Love again for fear of loss. To see your loss is to look upon Love. For what is a rose garden if not for the sweet moment it blossoms and the time you take for granted as dormant the bushes lay through the seasons until blossoms do again carry the sweet nectars blooming honey to your senses. Every rose before, all the memories attached and connected after reborn. What of summers torch. What of falls death, What of springs awakening, What of winters cold reset. What of humans that seed the slight fleeting passion of Love, caring not for the longing of the miss. So quick to blame, replace, divorce, fulfill, and act on every wish. I deserve it all. I want it. I need it. I will never forgive. I cannot wait as I long for revenge. I yes to want it all. The we run far behind from the I, yet as the tortoise and hare know all too well, we wins together forging into the past, present, and future, embracing not the insidious I, but welling forth the wondrous we.

We move as one. We can move mountains. We are never alone. You can buy for I even the great eye in the sky. We

break through the indignations of the sultans
sovereignty. I throws a stone. I want more.
Be not riddled with all the pain and pleasure
of I. Together we forge a vault of Love
unbreakable by the I of borrowed time.
Together the needs of many outweigh the
wants of few. Boundless oceans of still blue
waters, lakes pristine as melted knowing
cascading together, the wondrous array of all
the I knows not, and the I cannot behold
what the inner eye knows, that we walk the
path as we together never I alone. So put
down the stone, the phone, the cone, and
Jacobs jawbone.

      I am will never lead you astray. I am
will never force you to be. I am this. I am
that. I am you. Many times the I of time
has dwelled in the hearts of men. Many
times have the forgiven already been
forgave. One thing withstands the eye of
time, your sister, mother, father, and brother,
facing forwards striding together while not
looking back, then times curse will touch not
your essence. Temptation always starts ends
and begins with the eyes most cherished
song, I. Weave not the trickery slavery and
deception of time unto your inner eyes brow
for all the I wants is cleverly splashed

flashed and sassed in deceit. To seed and sow the we, is to love honor and care for each other. That is all there is. Nothing in time matters, we see it as just idle chatter. One we. One way. One light. Unto this day we are all born together free to pass out of the halls of time.

The same souls which believe not, scoff, and spit at my name. These same souls scream out crucify him, crucify him. The same souls took without giving. These same souls will line up to take the mark. These same souls upon my return will scream out in agonizing sorrow. Save us. Forgive me. We knew not. So sorrowful am I. So hungry am I. Please may I drink for drinkings sake. Many chances and pleas from above were given. Harkened the call then you did not. The harp played as you danced to the drum of war. Loud and haughty your prideful arrogance as break free unto your own creations did thee. It bringeth me great sorrow to watch as you remain in the clouds longing for mans cup of life. But unto me the great cup of knowledge, truth, and purity. Unto one another your sister and brother will the sweetest nectar of Love be full, filled, purified, restored, and renewed. Strong is your concrete, yet stronger the convulsing cracks born deep in the heart of the great mother. She will shake and convulse the likes of which hath never been seen by eyes before. Those that listen, drawn to higher safer grounds will they be. Those with sharp fangs and ravenous as a snake, drawn to the sands will they be, only to be swallowed up as the Angelic winged ones pick up and scour the seas for those pure of heart and full of forgiveness. I am my fathers father. I weep tears endlessly as continually there lust for horror fear and drunken gluttony carries forth creations which prey upon the innocent as they drink from the cup of fear.

Take ease and be of good character
for I forged the cup. I placed the ore as
sands of time pressured the pressures
creating all that glistens. I am felt, not seen.
I am moving in the cracks and crevices of
time forging a path of clarity and clear
precision so the light may shine unto the day
and day unto night. The wicked cast their
games under the cover of night to frighten
all those who toil under the sun to pass the
weary head unto the pillow at night. I shall
be uplifted and exalted by all those who
wish to defame, spit upon, and explain away
unto themselves that a maker exists not. My
joy and truth will spill forth unto this land
from the skies, the oceans, the volcanoes,
every fissure cracking will crack. The
penguins and polar bears will find an
abundant supply of food. Those dependent
on tree and jungle which you so easily cut
down, they too shall find renewed growth
and shelter. The gates of my house where
the prophets and scribes words hath been
stilted will be blown open and restored with
those bold and clever enough to seek within
following not that of the past.

Who so ever walketh with diligence humbly wanting only for others to know peace, they will be restored. Who so ever giveth thy last dime will be given an abundance of the heart. Who so ever heeds that what you get, is what is given, to them I will light the way. Be of sound judgment, glorify the sight of your hearts vision. Make it your mission to heed the call of hungry children, hurting elders, and those filled with confusion and pain.

Together the ship can be uplifted. Together the winds of change blow true and calm. Together the carnivorous find peace at the tree of life sprouting forth all the nutrition man needs to prosper, glow, and live long. Together those forces seen not by the simple eyes of men, toil endlessly to place foul dark roots into the wellspring of life. They will be cast out, forced to return home humbled, hungry, tired, and distraught. They, my creations as well, will be welcomed unto my gates, forgiven, returned, anointed, the endless well of love and life restored. There be no rest for the wicked, but as my prodigal sons return, only rest and forgiveness will they find. No judgment, no prison, no long standing suffering. Only penance, humility, grace, and restoration for now and forever until the next creation begins. For to love is to nurture, and to nurture is to calm, and too calm is to be patient, and to be patient is to forgive. To forgive is to be free.

There is only you in and of yourself. All questions, answers, truths, and knowledge are stored within. Eternally lay only you and yourself of this now, unto your heart waiting patiently the keys to the codex. In others strive to see, know, allow, and honor in every word, thought, movement, and action. Every longing desire thought and want leads external, a path to the grave. Seeking together as one, with joy, solidarity, and want of only togetherness, the doors of all open unto the sands of time flowing out in every direction the wisdom of total nothingness. To define judge and group people, bonds, nations, ownerships, and commonwealths, with numbers so high and words so profound, is to turn the back and slap away the hand of the highest maker. Exalted and carried home be those which open the pastures groves fields and spaces to the cold, weary, and drowning. If there be only you, how then can you ever experience, we, us, together, a flock united as a whole, an entire unit free of judgment doubt and limitation of mental mind. The amount of knowing contained within every mind of all beings is but a single color in the broad spectrum of my creation pallet. Know that in your knowing you know nothing. To reset the clock and move time to a standstill is a truth living in the codex of I am. I am you, made in the image of me, of this I am

so proud and so ashamed, as with the time
your gifted many pains hurts insults and
treacheries have I born witness to. Not one
tear or broken heart has gone unnoticed by
my hand eyes and heart. Heavy is my
burden as the resets, flashes, floods, and
gaseous storms wipe clean the slate as I
again take chalk to board, pencil to paper,
oil to canvas. My hand stretched unto you
waiting, coursing love steadily to all with
open hearts and calm loins which heed the
physical not. To consume is to be
consumed. To hurt is to hate. To take is to
be taken. To love is to know all you need.
See, breathe, feel calm water flowing
through your being. Run quickly from all
those alive and not hashing a plot to strangle
the roots grown deep in the great garden. I
allowed the snake unto Eve. I opened the
gate so it may slither in. All this have I done
to show you what is and is not. What should
and should not. What comes and then goes.
The bite of the viper sends venom unto all
parts. The knowledge of knowing leads the
path unto all paths which always as my
prodigals do you walk and returneth home.
I am that which made the garden and
fortified it with life. I am that same maker

that will seek to close, restore, and renew the
great garden, yanking out the asp, allowing
once again for the sheep to lay silent unto
the lion children among them playing,
learning, safe once more.

Be prudent and ever ready for the
coming for it may shine upon all from deep
within and far away. Narrow is the passage
and short is the way when you look but
calmly within to count the most sacred
treasure of all. Every man, woman, child,
and creepy crawling thing sharing the air,
water, earth, and fire, brought about by the
great fall. I will be your rock and steady
hand in torrential currents and rapids as you
navigate the all. I will sustain you with
breath when you have none left. I will take
steps for you when no more can you walk. I
will calm the mind with hushing lullabies
when the frequent frequencies bombard your
mind, ear, and soul. I will make warm and
whole the hurt, tired, homeless, and
addicted. I will bring to the highest
mountain and deepest inner cave, peace,
freedom, steadiness, and nurturing. I have
not forsaken you. I have opened your eyes
to that which you had not eyes to see. You

will find your way home and unto you,
amongst all your enemies and injuries a
table shall be set, and you will know Love,
Light, Truth, Calm, and the all. Give us
today and care not for tomorrow for in the
moment will you find internal life eternal.

      Ever do you worship sound symbols
vibration and chords. Ever do you look for
ambient noise to open the gates for a peak or
glare to warm your cold spheres. Doth stars
and harps spark upon the swallows chords a
melodious grace so sweet, leading you left
in a deep delta state, we say yes of course,
but be aware that to move past the green
serpents sting, to unwind that which you are
wound with, a totality of inner knowing true
to you is the only sound needed to make the
grand escape from this fiery place. Isis
chords so enchanting and lulling, but a
lullaby doth put one to sleep, a melodious
chant the true maker it is not. For who truly
does the bell in that steeple toll. Position the
people in a studious station then together
ornate a nice little cake do they bake.
Sphere there, sound there, cleverly crafted
creations of the mighty snake slithering.
Truly examine those who commissioned that

joyous snake cupped vibrant glass art lest ye
find yourself lost in the melodious void
drunk on the champagne brain, beset with
sound, glowing to bed with fortuitous
yearnings as oh, all those vibrations will
surely see me to heavens door. Yet be aware
that on that boat called life lay many
melodious sounds settling, cleverly placed
upon the altars star laden space. We ask
thus, is it truly a church if there be no bell in
the steeple. Honor the vibratory sounds all
living beings make, but always be guarded,
as the great snake surely flourishes in states
of sounds which all things make. Worship
this not for it is yet another fraction of a
fractal distilled in an essence to keep you
lingering thus. In total dismay do we cry
every day as you spend countless hours
looking to sound symbol and distance, when
for only a penny and deep breathe, inside
your heart to soul make haste, and you will
find no sound or bellows oh dear fellow.
How quickly the ghost will fool confuse and
steal if unto musical vibration you go for
worship and grace, what a slap in the face.
To be in tune with the true source of living
eternal light requires not a long organ pipe
or purring melodious hum. With yourself do

you hum, and with yourself you will stay in splendid array, beaming beacons, quiet calm receptors, guarding the lighthouse, becoming simple calm elegant way showers. The symbols of sounds will transport you away to a far off place leaving a serene expression upon your face. But have you given any thought to those which molded crafted and connected the stars waves with the sounds of the seven days. To lay down your burden is to deeply know that to look is to listen, as the stars do they glisten, but in every lullaby goodnight the mother she knows that to sleep a child goes, yet hard to watch as every chatter chord harmony and bellowing beatbox vibrates the great mirror for you to consider that set up as a test it all cleverly has been, and we say unto you: A man most deaf has an easier step back home up above, not splintered in echo sounds that surely come from bellow. Do really you think that the nun with her sparrow gets closer to the all when she hears the pipes call. For you to consider before you shoot another bow at a quiver, pulsing sounds vibrations to open the spaces in between. With this you should not tamper lest ye find the king of snakes beating down your front

door as harnessing clever chaos cords of
chords sounds has this fine fiendish foe.
Mastery of vibration and harmonies they
have, trickling narrow bands into your brain
and your mothers too. You may want to
manage what waves float unto your brain,
for the hood of the cobra will take but it all,
pulling downward, deep descent you will
fall, directly into your brain, such a delving
theta thought train. So be calm, quiet, and
true, so no devious snake can pull upon you.

There once was a mighty seafaring whale that would jump play and splash, needing at times to come up for air. This mighty whale with his huge splashy tail had fun splashing the whole boat that on the sea would he float. Filtering out plankton, teeth made of ivory baleen, he swam about leaving love in his wake spreading joy the whole way. A long healthy life would he live with his tribe connecting the love and good wishes left all along the shores by dolphins and other mer creatures. Along they swam filtering out more than just small plankton, oh no, you see whales filter out bad dreams, hurts, fears, and misfortune, a most noble job for certain. Love was all this king of the sea knew, and Love is what was born renewed from all the fear and unclear uncertainty born most astute from the eyes, ears, and whispers, of the people he looked after, never asking for anything in return as he floateth about turning so true, a most elegant vision for any lucky enough to behold his full frontal abode to unfold his big caring soul. His back so strong, and his skin home for so many little creatures, what a loving giving feature for such a large beautiful elegant creature. Just because you cannot see him, does not mean he is not there, caring, sharing, and bellowing, a magic creature for share so aware. In his eyes, they saw some caring but mostly not. The humans and people he so connected to, whether they knew it or not, dumped and pumped small to large pieces and parts of shattered hurting and discarded plastic again and again in the ocean where he did swim. Very hard to tell the difference between plastic and plankton was it for him as unnatural creations of men polluteth the bath in which he did swim. Near some places that he floated his eyes would burn and his skin would itch because yuck nasty water bleached toxic and yellow constantly poured out from the people causing hurt to this fine fellow. But patient as ever and noble was he, able to handle most with glorious glee. So forgiving, caring, sharing the sea was he, never angry about anything as he floated about filtering out all the hurt and uncaring. But a lot he was wearing, never did he lose his joy, always he arose giving his mighty tale a splashing splendorous pop.

But a turn for the worse as he could not quench his thirst. All of the hurting anger and uncaring was weighing him down from all the biting hating punching and tearing from those that toss trash and others onto the ground. But strong he was in spirit, and faith he had in the people, that one day they would see the rain filled with acid and the poison gross nasty eeking and leaching, slowly choking the vast life filled ocean. A big smile he kept on his face, waiting, loving, wishing for all to stop throwing out waste and to always forgive, looking out for your mother, knowing in your heart that the whale also is your brother. Try as he may, slowly moving with rigorous might, but the tiny shattered pieces built up, and the plastic particles grew slowly, as it all settled in his belly. His eyes grew foggy from far reaching fertilizer that slowly ate away at his delicate sway. But his heart remained true, as heavier denser and slower he began to move. Hard to filter the heavy hatred by taking it into the deep blue when you are heavily burdened with particle pieces of broken hearts and plastic keepsakes that end up in the big blue lagoon.

But the whale never faltered, he never blamed. So strong was he that easy it would be to flip over the trawler boats whose nets ensnared his fishy friends. But

ever humble was he, as he swam on warning
all he could to flee the nets and oxygen free
spots that came to upwash the smart gentle
loving nurturing creatures born in safe blue
water nestled in deep cold places so rest they
could find.

       Days turned to months, as months
turned to years, and heavily bogged down
with heart hurting was he with tears in his
eyes. He had in his tank one last breach, one
glorious gigantic giant splash, so he
gathered all he could muster from down
deep in Joneses locker, and he pulled all the
hurting, all the uncaring, all the not sharing,
and with all his might after telling all his
fishy friends goodbye, he swam straight up
faster and faster, his heart full of grace but
burdened with hate until the surface he
breached, so far up in the sky he flew,
gravity not he knew, and his big heart laden
with all those pieces burst forth into a
million zillion particles of Love. To this day
when you look up after it rains you see all
those wishes and pieces in a splendorous
array that even to this day, we call the
rainbow. My Love, your Love, the wells
Love, four always and forever.

I Love. I care. I share. I do not look to ensnare. I take just what I need. I am soft and cuddly like a big teddy bear. I give and give and give. I see within others myself. I forgive knowing that forgiveness is the sweetest music of all. I want of todays bread todays rain todays lessons and todays truths focused not upon the past or the rains next weeks storm bringeth. I see that which I have seen and heard before. I need that which I see around myself. If I see but one tree blossoming and sit upon and under it day in and out then I will know of patience, strength, and calm. If upon the boxed creation of men I see hurt war suffering hatred judgment, and disharmony, then of these will mine eye and soul become. I am what I speak say and scream for unto you is given exactly that which proceeds out of your mind, mouth, heart, and body. I am a reflection of all I had been, all I see, and that which my parents and elders tell me to be. I am the soft spoken compassionate joyful caring giving, nurturing calm gentle waters of nourishing light, to change and extinguish the fires set by wasteful arrogance, intolerance, hatred, and better thens. I give unto others that which I am given freely, co creating with my fellow brothers and sisters upon the Fabric of Life.

The Spirits of lust and denial spinning about like a pendulum swings, whisps silent sayings into the ears of many the learnings misguided to feed the banks trust. Fortress square in perfection, the scream it is a must. But what a fuss, all hath trusted, in God we must muster. To have what we need and get what we want in the almighty dollar we long for and lisp on with lust. The forked hissing tongue giving to fees and misguided erroneous deeds. In the trust we must stay, in the banks trust we delight, love of safety, bottomless ocean fathoms so deep, pockets so dense, the hum and purr of those few fat cats delights. How cleverly divided amongst themselves they do whisper, all the while a twisty turn in the road ahead driving long term dark agendas with twisting twiddling riddled nefarious memes as all they plan and think about is to win.

But what of giving back, what of sharing even one quarter of what you hold in your stash. Fame, grain, jewels, trains, planes, boats, moats, and even love of lingering ghost, is that what you love the most. To the great wide eyed owls of the night do you give thanks and honor, asking for the dark vision to pierce through the night. What is it that you so long to see in the night. Should not your eyes rest weary to slumber. Should not your dreams well up as springs as you rest in the between. How tirelessly you slumber through the night, casting your nefarious wickedness to smear about your vengeance. Cold cowards you must be, waiting until someone falls weary to night after another day of hard earned coin for your banks as they slumber silently, asleep in the flickering false fake dream forged frantically with heavy furious thunder. So blessed and so chosen we know where we are going. Up on high into the clever counting cloud wearing the Torahs shroud while our Kings and Master makes waste to this desolate barren place. The acts of a few, the supreme wealth of the wicked sows wantonness waste driving destruction upon the great mother with devious plunder. Diamonds so large they burden the hand. Boats so grand they easily are stuck in the sand. The true ark is coming for all of those

eternally becoming and so stunning it will
be when suddenly like a cat stuck in a tree,
they pray to their big night eye god that
preys in the night. Heard the screams they
will not. Surely, I say that as the sun rises in
the West and falls in the East you and your
cohorts will be stuck in the soot left over.
Red rover range rover will not you surely fly
over to free my foot. Stuck in the trench and
stench of war you will be. Burdened with
chains of avarice and power in confusion
will your path always lead. How hearty and
boisterous you do gloat as upon the seven
seas you do float. Slurping suckling
cackling and laughing, drunken hedonist
delight as you worship night and sleep
through day. Laughing hyenas perched
upon high as you pray words of the past to
her of the night laying down blooded bone
and windswept swords drenched in dark lies
of twilight. So bright and so shiny if only I
could cram into that hiney whispers the dark
honey plumber. In the shadow of night is
where they partake of this cowardly delight.
All hath sinned and fell from grace yet you
seem to have fallen flat on your face into
and upon the magic toads pond. Tasted it all
you have. Drank drunken golden drinks

with many Kings hath the proud bold rich
and afflicted.

      We say unto you, and it has been
written, it be better to lay cold and dreary
among the drug addicts sick and weary to
share but one dried up crumb for they I will
reach and save. But smite far out in the
night which will give me no delight all those
blown in self serving snow for I see the
heart of the wicked and give chase with the
most glorious ticket. Your trip is booked.
Your room laden with the fallen rose petals
of suffering which you took from so many.
The table is set, the silver polished, as
descend you will into the abysmal night with
all the kings of night to which you give
credence and take call, casting upon the
world your foul intention giving yourself
pleasure and delight. No words can describe
how alone and entangled you shall feel
when cast off and away to your deepest
darkest fear, and there you will stay chained
to the vast oceans deep bottom, beaten sick
starving and downtrodden until I see fit to
acquit.

You see in the world all that you want kneading more. Hard to retain your Faith when all you witness in this place is hurt pain violence and forgotten Grace. The sword it does cut, the diamonds they do glisten, but take to this call so when you stumble you do not fall. In this shiny maze all on fire and set ablaze your Faith is being tested. I heed hear and listen unto your call. How could the maker, a most glorious baker, not run to the call of the innocent that fall by the hands of the wicked. The pain from the stain has been taken in vain. It hath not changed as these words the counseling leaders in time will not coerce as all the paint in the world will not be enough to restore the Sistine chapels most sacred of scenes for to better or worse you speak on a curse. With zest and haste, you run to consume all which once had a face. If in the flesh you give grace, then of flesh you will stay, free will set ablaze. For those that see all creatures have a loving heart just as thee, for them I make pace and hurry open the gate. You run and you fall. You witness all you need in your mall. In my house it is safe so in my house I will stay. This man and that girl cried up in a knot screaming in

the sorrow of shiny things in a shop. You
will stumble and fall. You shall walk after
crawl. Every step you take in this place a
great wave doth it make. Return to you it
will always makes haste as together you
create in this place. So mysterious to us
whilst you spit curse and thrust giving
credence unto thee and not for another as
yourself you see not in that others face. Not
much else to say except lifes living moments
today, fleeting as they may be are there as a
sign to see past your own present design,
resigning you from time to loves calm gentle
kiss, a path to loves eternal bliss without a
knock pinch or hiss, for built in this design
is your grand reception beset with eternal
redemption if past the vision of self serving
joy you make haste, then calmer loving
nurturing waters will find you. In this place
to the grand staircase make haste for the seal
will open as the words will be spoken. The
prophets will see the coming calamity
foretold to thee as with the sheep he will lay
on a soft bed of hay for past all the hurt was
he so very tested, yet still, he found in
himself his faith most uplifted. To him, she
did show that only a friend is a foe. I do
hope you listen to your heart as it whispers

so gently at night without a care or a fright.
Your new home have I made, safe sweet
dreams of eternal play will you lay, as cast
into the void to hurt the innocent no more
those of worldly ways which I made as I
violently shake to break free from the mold
those which bottled and sold to the highest
bidder the elixir of quitters. I am the hardest
hitter of this you will know for in the peaks
of the valleys for which water never flows I
will make it snow. Those with no self
esteem in them I will gleam as tomorrow
today every sinner and saint for all will I
make the snake lay down beside still waters
its fangs and venom no more as I look to
restore that which I love evermore as I await
at the gates for you to make the leap of faith
that Indy did make knowing not what you
see but with patience humility and penitence
will you be as I come to collect the flock and
reset the clock to renew and make true this
my promise to you. To Mia Amore, I do so
Love and adore tears and bloodshed no more
this my promise to restore.

Unto thine own heart be true. Speak softly and gently among those loud and proud. Making your point, though perfect and sweet to your ears, may be dull, void, and lifeless, if that point is sharpened to a tip, and that tip glistens as pearl white snow or be shiny as gold, but a point becomes painted into form through spoken words turned to nail, knife, or fashion. What be a point if unto another your fellow brother it hurts. Studious and courageous the man who looks not to ensnare with promise of pasture, profit, or air swept house soffit. You have never seen winds of the like which are coming, turning nothing back to nothing, please hear when I say, molded you were from one ball of clay and back you will go in the blink of an eye, and to some it will be such a surprise, to most a welcome call, for waiting patiently as the deserts for rain hath been this eons stall. Look around you this day and try for a moment to remember play. A great star is set ablaze just as it was over Bethlehem before, and it comes to you from a great distance offshore. If you look with squinted eyes you will know before the tinted tides become shifted to knock down your door. What a fright to see the lands seas and skies light up at night. How far down will you go. How much fight is left until you fight no more. How deep into earths crust can you drill. How many of those mind numbing pills must you take. How much Life must you consume from cows pigs and chickens until you see they too glisten with Life. How many times will you beat and cheat on your wife. How many grapes, their life did it take, for those bottles of wine you drink at dinner time. How much hurt beat broken and sore must you endure, until at the chorus door you listen to gentle chords calm nurturing knock at your hearts front door. How many tremendous parties with all of this, them, those, and that, will you hold until you break out of your mold.

It should come as no surprise that to walk in a straight hath the same direction as walking in a curve. The bluebirds round egg and the eye of the hedonistic heathen hold within the same quantity. If your eye leadeth you astray pluck it out and make an omelet some would say. A deeper truth more profound is the torment lies and inaccuracies being fed unto your crown. To see oneself as a King is to see oneself as every King before now and after. In times lock the trapping embrace made so delicately into the new wives pink frilly lace. Embrace that which guardeth the eye and also the egg for the two are the same. Both delicate intricate and full of life. Both so eager to experience. The egg of a lizard so heavy and thick, the eye of a human so quick to become sick, with a heavy heart the two spliced together make for a devious art. Nefarious means to longer life so serene. The science queen with her three ornate beakers, her long reach into deep pockets has made it so no one can stop her. We hope and pray for the sake of you all that these eggs stay sacred, but the lizards do not stop, and they surely do not listen. Twisted into tormented lies riddled in hopes of longer

linear liquid light bodies. Morphing and
twisting atomic minute measurements
making milky the void and hath left us so
annoyed. True life everlasting they scream
out and chant while fight to the death they
do while nestled high in the clouds. A sad
day for all when on earth they evolve
backwards past crawl to slithering slide, a
hissing event for certain to attempt and stop
the progression of all. I know of one
hundred monkeys older than that and wiser
than you that will unleash sovereign truth
unto your slithering seat as backwards to
primordial you stay as you fall. For us, it
has been but an instant, but you dig look
observe and listen to those who are truly
your captor for what you know not is they
cannot survive without your sweet egg to
flop from the badlands from whence they
did come to fool trick and deceive those who
always want in longing for more.

        But we ask you thus: what happened
in Sodom and Gomorrah. What happened to
Solomons sweet song. What does it say in
the twenty third Psalm. What happened
when Saul through faith turned inward to
Paul. The past streams forth repetition as

tracks run in only one direction but straight
is curved and around is within as a pinprick
draws the blood to drops on the mud as all
the wildfowl and great beast are saved from
the flood. We look on the people and those
ringing bells in the steeple, who art those to
reseed this time as a most calamitous fortune
is headed your way. It would all come to a
stop if to bed you put your intricate plot.
The architect defines the light bearing
receptors and they are made as an innermost
reflector but if back to living in moats you
must go who are we to stop you, go ahead
be again the gazpacho.

Why eat toast when you can chew on
people. Why just be you and let them be
them when you can crawl in a cave and live
in the sand. We have seen how it ends and
we know where it is headed when
backwards you trace rewriting the code that
gives you a face. It looks like a storm is
most certainly coming for you seem to have
fun unzipping while you unbutton. Love
will make no mistake while you so
treacherously make the terrible mistake of
pining splicing and pruning that most sacred
and dear so you can glow most austere. We

sit dumbfounded and baffled watching you figure out Jacobs ladder. The climb to the top waits not for the flop. Gambling with the code is a simple deed you should stop as you hide your egg ovary placental lab underneath that sweatshop. The lease is no longer renewed. The founders are coming, and we like not what we see you becoming. The window curtain pulled tight children tucked in at night, yet blinded you stare, woefully unaware with window blinds open wide. Lookout in the shore for answers and more, but the show is over, the curtain is called, the show must go on but without you singing the final song.

Did you know that words when spoken if not from the heart and soft spoken can hurt people places and things. Be most leery about every word said unto your brother. Speak foul of them not. Use not your device to start fires and throw dirt into cooked rice. You see most barely make it in this day and age and a kind word or lovely thought may in them help to imbue grace. This is what it means to live in true faith. Rebuke your brethren with grand exalted thought, we think not. If in heart you are wearing gentle soft spoken love that knows not comparing the will to love all burns in through and beyond any not caring yelling or swearing.

Easy to grab, the anger lingers. Sit in what bothers to let go of the fodder and the anchor will release. Free you will be forever if unto your fellow man you speak of good tidings and great joy, not of I have this greatest pleasant toy. Things are just stuff and you cannot fit any of it on the bus to where we are going. So important to know that your unspoken thoughts have great impact. If you harbor anger and be grudgingly think nasty thoughts of a terrible

nature heaviness lands on that persons heart
and if enough people do it then they might
just ruin another gentle vessel, a harsh
burden to carry.

　　　　Think thoughts of caring and
sharing. Wish not for the downfall of the
world or calamity for another as deep and
vast is the ocean of thought and heavy the
world has become with critical vengeance
fueling painful hurtful thoughts. Think of
others as they think of Love. Dispel with
anger and vengeance for this burdens the
soul. Your animals, loyal friends as they are,
harbor nothing but Loving jovial fun joyful
play until locked in a box all day then they
too have angry thoughts, for no bird animal
or person should ever be locked away in a
painful box made of words and thoughts.
Both carry your true intentions out in every
direction.

　　　　Be of pure mind and body. Watch
not scary things or be shocked by clever
memes. Fools runneth quick to grab sticks
of thoughts and words of stone to aim
quickly for a dose of fear but it leaves
behind an awful smear as hurt just continues
to volley and ride the trolley of life. Life

takes time to make just like a rising cake so care about your words and look upon every thought so you do not get trapped and stuck in your own anger box. If back around it comes sharing Love it is so sweet and true, but if square angled and scary a notion it doth carry your shine most exalted to the land of uncaring. We see all the thoughts and every hurt that keeps you trapped in the box. We are always there waiting hands outstretched wings ready to cover the soul and mend the heart when out of the dark you take just one step. Together is the best way to do it with friends family and fishes too, your friends most exalted as out of the fray you start skipping, jumping, dancing and loving. You see no matter how clever that self made box of uncaring the pure stream of joyous melodious loving thought will melt through that heavy box leaving you calm cool and collected in control of your words thoughts and actions. Do you see anything square on the earth or in the air. We think not, so be ever aware speaking loving thoughts and prayers to never again find yourself stuck in the cocreative box forged of lies hate and mistrust lest you lose everything in that square vault of misguided trust. All your fair weather friends that drink all your gin in your perfect glass square box will care for you not if you did not have this on that in those with them. A true friend will always invite you in, but you need not fuss of those that care only for what stinks of uncaring locked away in a vault or a trust in that banks square box. Circle, circle, without a dot and poof no more locks in a box tied to what happens in the clock. Just fun in the sun a most joyous occasion as together we strive standing true with purified thoughts wanting for not lest forever you drown in that square box upside down forever and always in the games that you play with spoken words and thoughts so you can fit in that fake silly box.

There is but only one. From this one
all life sprang forth. The one is the host of I
Am. The I am is dipped in the deep pools of
knowing the perception of self in others.
The one of I am is steeped in choice and free
will. How mighty and courageous be the
Lion, and yet he sleeps all the same as others
at night, quiet, calm, resting and vulnerable.
The spring of all from the one has drunk
water from every corner, of every pool,
stream, river, and cave, from the farthest
corners of all time in every space. So
expansive and vast is the truth of things seen
streaming forth the gates are needed no
more. There is a fragile hum of sacred space
and it can be found taken cared for
acknowledged, and tossed away to float unto
places unseen, and to wither away beside a
cold rock with no light, shivering, releasing
its essence smell and hum back into the
place of origin. All flowers fall from the
vine. All sinners and saints will fall upon
the sword of one nestled in self made nests
of perception crafted of I am forged in the
great hum nestled in the sands of time. The
hallways and corridors of life exist as
impressions upon the chambers of knowing.
A rock falleth from a high ledge and roles

the path woven around, besides, over, between, through whatever lay in its path leaving its impression upon all these things for which it touched bent and came into contact with. The rock knows only its current form and the heaviness calcified within that form, many days and nights, many cycles of rain and dry, many continuations of pressure and time will one day reform, return, and renew every mold divot impression and heaviness the rock took part in, remolding the vast hum of regeneration.

  I am but the one rock cascading forth bellowing out the torrential hum as it falls tumbles cracks open and is reborn. The ashes formed of its other fallen friends as together they do rumble and tumble tapping against the large ledge, smoothed etched and primed by the torrential waters carrying mightily these stones as they journey together being changed formed molded and perfected, to yet one day know form not, only the sweet hum of the one. Verily we would say that one drop of rain, one leaf, one blade of grass, one pebble, one small unseen minute particle, together as one they are mighty and forthright, swelling the stream to a river giving rise to the highest peaks and form unto the lowest valleys. To know the I am is to know the one. To know yourself as one drop of rain among the torrent rushing all around you is to truly be the hum of life. The bird sees in one stick potential, strength, and togetherness, to protect its eggs. The snake digs but one dark deep hole and knows only the protection of its skin in this one place. The squirrel picks up but one acorn in its clasping hand to add unto its stash of abundance. The solitary drop of rain falls into the lake, the lake being but one body of water itself. The eagle focuses upon one fish in the one lake its eye set upon and focused on yet one thing. The rabbit pulls but one carrot from the ground totally content as it sits consuming but one thing. The little boy picks up but one stone to skip across the water in the joy of that one moment. Doth in that moment he knoweth of that rocks long journey, or of the many drops of rain it took to form the lake. The one of many comes together to form the choice of a moment and this is the love grace truth purity and form of the I am. To know yourself in that moment as one thing comprised of many things is to grace the highest ridge, and to float the vast sea of togetherness. A drop of creation you are, narrowly minding meandering and moving through the great halls of form and existence molding and being molded as one in the eye of I am drifting past all gates boundaries barriers and veils set forth along your path as you perilously cascade down the river of one headed home to dance the boundless leap of infinite a wash in the great hum of One.

A man most clever sat one day upon an old stone. He asked the rock, teach me all you have known and seen over the thousand years of rain, famine, drought, starry nights and daybreak sunsets, flowering trees, and birds chirping full of early morning glee. What sayeth you rock, the man beggeth still, tell me of night and day, speak to me, are you longing for legs so you may run and play. Such pity I have for you that in this same place you sit with no mouth to speak and no arms to hug. How can you see all the glorious splendor of the world when eyes you have not. So much I could teach and share with you stone rock, why will you not just speak up so we may share this wine I spilled within my gold laden embellished cup. Oh, rock, how I pray and ask that you sprout arms, legs, mouth, eyes, and face, so we can share a loving embrace. The man with his foolish pride and haughty knowing cleverly hinged to his side, looketh down again and asketh the rock once more, teach me about the all mighty, show me the all. If you could only listen to my words and heed my beckon call, then surely and assertively I would drink of your stoic stone knowledge. The stone answered not, and the man ever more clever in his foolishness poureth out his sullied wine upon the rock and spat upon it, cursing, yelling thus, why will you not share your tale, tell me what you know or I will be forced to leave you and go. Angry at himself and upset the man sat down beside the rock crying, feeling ashamed at his actions towards the stone. As he sat weeping puppy dog tears soaking the ground, he realized at that moment how much the silent gentle rock had taught him by being still, allowing, speaking not.

The man over the years grateful for the lessons and wisdom the rock shared returned to the stone whispering his every secret, cried time and time again, sleeping deep nurturing sleep beside the stone in the warm sun nestled silently together like a bird in a tree. The day came when the man could barely walk, his eyes grew weary of the sun, and the fields grew no more vine due to famine and drought. He, moving ever so slow in need of a cane to walk, sat down beside his old friend hugging the stone tight whispering, I love you good night. The man fell into a deep sleep never to awake again and the rock wept watery tears from its eyes as he would miss the stories, growth, hardship, and tales of joy the man shared. I am man. I am stone. I am calm. I am quiet. I am the all. Be still as the stone, and you will find I am in your heart.

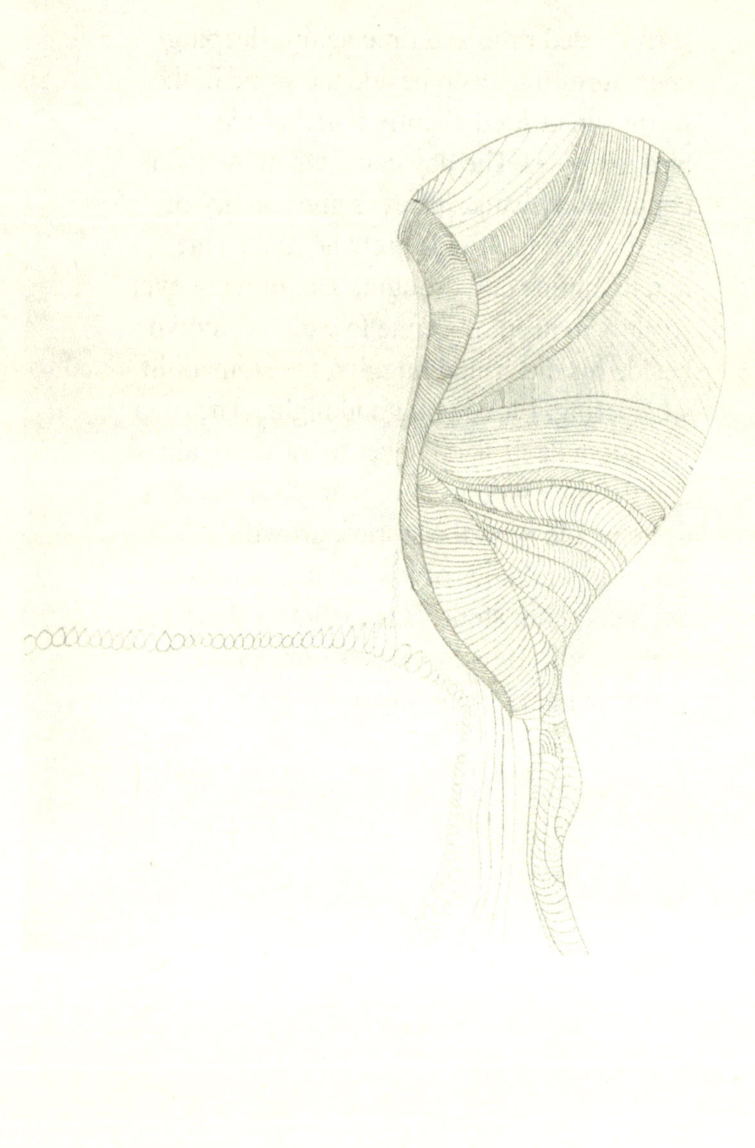

Our Love makes us strong. Our
Love is seeded in calm truth and flowing
compassion. Our Love moves together,
united as one. Our Love never gives up.
Our Love leaps the endless oceans of time.
Our Love is slow to anger and quick to
forgive. Our Love flows eternally through
the sands of time. Our Love feeds the
hungry and warms the cold. Our Love
blinds the angry wicked and vindictive. Our
love is never alone. Our Love does not
compete. Our Love fills stadiums with
Love, not war. Our Love meets with the
Love of all others. Our Love is sober in
humble continuity. Our Love does not have
the word quit or give up in its vocabulary.
Our Love moves the hands of time. Our
Love lays hands of joy upon the sick and
weary. Our Love does not confuse or judge.
Our Love moves mountains. Our Love
creates more Love. Our Love shakes the
fear from the soul. Our Love feeds life unto
more life. Our Love is wise, kind, quiet, and
steady. Our Love remains human. Our
Love is a beacon of hope shining in the pitch
black void of night. Our Love lays down the
seed and waits to reap that which we sow.
Love is the fruit of our labor. Our Love

drenches the harshness of the stealers of dreams. Our Love trust not in computers. Our Love beats down the door of the Lairs where the Liars live. Our Love is an old pair of cotton overalls with dirty knees and farm muddy boots. Our Love never wears shoes that hurt our feet. Our Love does not tell women to cut their body hair off, paint their faces in poison, or looks to quiet their precious voice. Our Love tells not our men that to be men they must be willing to die for the cause. Our Love speaks out to honor truth above all else. Our Love is what truth tellers have died for. Our Love needs no limits. Our Love has no unfriend button. Our Love honors the boundary between the dead and the living. Our Love is afraid not of death. Our Love respects our Mothers and honors our Fathers. Our Love shares with others. Our Love is soft, gentle, and caring as the Arms of Angels. Our Love speaks up in authenticity always. Our Love jumps out of the rails bound not in Space or Time. Our Love keeps promises. Our Love is free to all. Our Love breaks the mold. Our Love finds its way to every empty heart. Our Love leaves no man behind. Our Love is stronger when we move together in unity surrounded by truth. Our Love sees no color, gender, or sexual orientation. Our Love does not need a building or cross to capture its strength. Our Love calms the oceans. Our Love lights the path before you. Our Love moves frozen hearts. Our Love opens every vault. Our Love sees, nurtures, and calmly cares for your every fault. Our Love is tender and true. Our Love breaks down walls with a thunderous roar. Our Love will never require from you something. Our Love goes on forever. Our Love is tender and sweet. Our Love gives haste unto your feet. Our Love asks for little and gives back much. Our Love restoreth the soul. Our Love calms the oceans and the winds. Our Love warms the cold and forgives the wicked. Our Love does not place bets on war angry people. Our Love tends to those who have not. Our Love calms the hand and restoreth the heart. Our Love honors all that breathe life. Our Love is kind caring and true. Our Love lays down beside you in green lush safe pastures. Our Love speaks truth unto the heart of man. Our Love just is. Our Love leaves flowers of caring upon the heart of man. Our Love never leads the children astray. Our Love

believes in the power of Love. Our Love
will move you to tears. Our Love will rattle
your bones. Our Love is a nest of freedom.
Our Love knows not of uncaring. Our Love
is like a tree, unwaivered, steady, calm, a
safe place to be and rest. Our Love together
moves the mightiest mountain. Our Love is
rooted in faith, caring, compassion, and
wisdom. Our Love lives on the back of a
turtles shell. Our Love is green, balanced,
calm, and fierce as a mighty pandas big
heart. Our Love is fast zippy and free
defying gravity just like the hummingbird.
Our Love is the deepest Blue ocean in the
darkest of trenches. Our Love wears its
vulnerability without a care in the world.
Our Love is felt in every heart, everywhere,
in this world, and others. Our Love feeds
hope unto joy. Our Love is so much more.
Our Love does not know of the word quit.
Our Love never needs to throw a fit. Our
Love builds bridges over uncrossable
divides. Our Love seeks to cherish, honor,
adore, and restore, all that are lost and
ignored. Our Love shelters the meek and
weak. Our Love blooms blossoms of
blanketing courage, calm and content all
across the lands, oceans, mountains, rivers,

forests, peaks, and valleys. Our love is an eternal wellspring of life, flowing forth for all to see, hear, feel, and share.

Without your praise he most uplifted, his robes they will tatter, his followers will see how consumed and hurt was the earth at his lead, left in shattered torn remnants. Soft spoken at first as they lean in to listen as his words and crown of might do they glisten. Very few will see through his soft melodic prose as follow him anywhere off any cliff will they go. Teachings of anger and glorious banter until back into the ground will they all crawl for it is from whence they came. Practice not what he preaches as from the streets that he was uplifted will he run like a coward when walls are breached, and vineyards destroyed, as the farms and wells are no more. But foresee it he did and hoard all the resources has he. Dried milk figs and dates what a curious state. Foresee in the future the dreams showing him on a mission, names and blames he will befall, yet truth will be told so it can be seen by all. You can sign a petition, you can look and not listen, so hear the call and you need not fall into this ravenous trap beset all around

to tear, snare, leaving utterance bare, likes
trapping ensnare.

For miles snaking through wired
fences and concrete barricades will those
same loving people linger, for unto him they
will wait and beg to acquire for their disease
stricken vessel a dried up cake, so they may
have a tiny stake at the life they had before
which they found to be such a bore.
Supremely humbled by the trouble as to the
knees and faces will they go, precious water
tearing from the eye, shaken to the core, to
crumbling bones they will fall.

Look inside your heart. Listen to
your inner voice, it will cry out I am. Learn
what it means to Love with utmost esteem.
The wicked and sinners dressed up as
glorious winners will shrivel on the vine for
it is that created time. It is all that shares
with you, unto you, made in our image. It is
my endless wellspring of Love that I share
with you. The pen is truly mightier than the
sword. The waters of life from which light
and darkness are born will be purged and no
more. We have so much in store for all the
drops of life once restored to the authentic
state back to the road of less travel. Carry
no baggage, will we. Hearts glowing in the

continual stream of together. We create all
which we are, giving as we are given,
sharing as we have been shared with,
forgiving as we are forgiven. We mean you
no harm yet with your thoughts and voice,
you have made yourself into a farm.

I am the hand which prunes the tree.
I am that which will pluck the snake from
the garden. I am you and you are me and I
will do whatever it takes. I will wait for you
until the void of time itself glows no longer.
I am the beginning of the end. Look upon
your brother, and sister, fathers, daughters,
and mothers, see the sound the heart makes.
No face place make model or bottle will
cause you to falter when unto the joy and
grace of Love, will you make the blue jewel
shine far bright and wide for all to gloriously
behold one small drop of water flowing
eternally into the bucket when seeing the
truth of total trust. May your love flow as
an eternal wellspring of life. May you see
your path and know it is you who creates
your purpose. Gratitude my beloveds.
Grateful for all will lift you from the
constraints of time and free you from the
chains of gravity. Love is life. Life is grace
you give unto yourself. Grace flows freely

for all, you need only look upon the grain filled vanity in the sands of time and your light will brightly dance with all other lights as I long for your return, and will rest not until the weak, children, and troubled mothers, live not in a place of fear and want.

The end is near, the fall is coming, the reveal of revelation cometh. Where fear, peace. What was hate, now love. What was a query, is now faith. I am close. I am love. I am grateful for the lessons. I am the wind that flames the fire of life. I am the water in your mothers womb. I am the fixed point of forgiveness shaken down, tossed forth all around in all the spaces in between, seen and unseen. I will undo all that I hath created if unto grace you look not upon. Let your little light shine to be seen for all time so you may know, be, give, and cherish.

Why follow in the foolish mans footsteps when off a cliff those steps do take. Why look upon the Iron gate hoping for a glance of those which propose to be great. Why look above and not below. Why look to the great teachers of old, toth, hermes, and all of those. It lies within all that which you need to know. Why hit with a stick or throw a fast pitch when focused away are they. Why ride around time and again in a circle. Why worship royalty in the color purple. Why wish upon a shooting star to wonder of that which you already are. Why look out upon the constellation so great for answers about your faith. Why want for not tearing apart that which lies suffering upon the cross. Maltese of four, crossed images of him hanging upon your door. Cover not these upon your heart. Tied died glass of days long forgotten the stories myths parables and creeds of days long begotten. Why drink the sacred frozen snow of days long ago hoping to find calm when all you do is stubble your already swollen toe. Why run the blood of youth unto your veins to help you try to feel sane. Why plan for tomorrow when you can do for today. Why relish in the wisdom of deep thought

when it all one day ends up in the burial
plot. Why crave a thing so icky when your
lungs are left sticky. Why drink the wine
and roast the swine consumed upon tables
made of pine. Why bathe in flowers and
indulgent idle chatter. Why do you feel as if
something you said was of such great matter.
Why pour more wine into the already drunks
cup. Why receive when you can give. Why
try when you can do. Why hate when you
can Love. Why toil about all day to come
home and linger upon the soft gluttonous
throne. Why always in a race to win if
winning means another must lose. Why go
to places of mall which are constant
reminders of that which causes stumble and
fall. Why give unto yourself anger, hate,
and discord, when you can give yourself
grace and compassion. Why linger in dark
confusing substance filled dens with little
light that cause all to fall. Why always curse
my name and doubt my existence when
never are you for one solidarity moment
quite enough to feel, look, and listen to my
voice, whispering timeless truth to calm
your soul and quench your thirst. Why hate,
what hath that ever given you but more hate.
Why wear a mask, label, belief, color, or

symbol, if it causes you and others to be separate or feel shame. Why lust for tomorrow when you can be all today.

How clever art thou in your ambitious creations. One Two Three, ABC, the first thing taught for you to see, know, and form thought. The arrogant heads held high in such pride of learning bots and techno wizards. Pruned face with utter disgrace when there created space worketh not by my hand and grace. Try so much with discord disgust and mistrust those who command the principalities of air and dust. Oh how they long to see the sights of the world. But we sayeth thus, if to drops in your bucket you make such a fuss, be sure to share with others, all your sisters and brothers, for great is our wrath and heavy the hand which smashes every bucket. The drops of Jupiter fallen once again unto the sacred halls of the great trust. You are already forgiven. You need only forgive yourself then in your heart find forgiveness for your fellow man, seeking not with your eyes, and hearing not with your ears, all the things, wants, wishes, and desires of the world. Eeeny, meenie, miny moe, catch a number by its toe if it should holler let it go then back to dust it will surely go.

They make promises, agreements, contracts, and guarantees. They hand out more minutes, time ticking away, the chase of forever always marching forward. They carry only what they can, quick to drop anything and anyone in the pursuit of more. They afford certain privileges to the few while taking from so many. They trench, hide, dig, fortify, and make heavy doors to keep safe strongholds. Fist gripping golden embellishments preserved in deeply dug airtight mountain vaults. They toil endlessly to downtrodden, confuse, and tarnish the tender hearts of all. They relish the relics and things of the dead as they chase the blood filled cups of the past. They know not and care not for your name, place, or presence, as they labor continually to preserve the palace castle and fame. They speak not themselves, safely nestled behind vipers, tricksters, and those with tongues of silver as doubt confusion separation threats bribery and deceit cast thick hazy clouds upon all that bear witness. They fly faster, further, quicker, making every effort to escape the natural pull and forces of creations spin. They take many substances and drink many things while surrounded by those who lavish praise. They toil endlessly in thought to drown out the loving voice after smacking away time and time again the patient, loving, outstretched hand of completion rest and forgiveness. They yell out to any that would have ears and listen, look at all the good I hath done, look at all the lands I own, and trees which bear fruit. Look at this and that and these, how full is my cup, how great am I, as they look only to glorify themselves, tempting the foolish eyes and drunken lips of whispering harlots which revel in gossip deceit trickery and misguided steps.

I am that place where the two ticking hands cross paths. I am the blood stained sheets of innocence far gone. I am the golden bars hoarded, killed for, and plotted against by those whose eyes have turned solid upon its splendid haze. I am the two sisters sharing side by side and together do laugh, love, and cry. I am the gates of eternity nestled between, throughout, and outside of time. I am the forged iron stake of war on which you hang the heads of your enemies. I am safety, you need not fearfully fret for that which you cannot control. My hand is upon everything. I will see to it that your captors, the liars idolaters and whore mongers, are seized captured tried and caged for their ravenous ways. I am that who takes from the rich and giveth unto the poor. I am your long lost friend that waits patiently for your call. I am the gatekeeper. I steady the steps strides and race of all that heed my call. I am comfort for the fatherless son who looks upon the wolves and lions as they tarry about consuming all which they see. I am the keeper of my brother and the calming hands of a worried mother. I am the hand that breaketh down the cold wall between father and son. I am that which tears the tongue from the deceivers face. I am the peace and joy you pray and sow upon your fellow man. I am the pride of arrogant haughty men. I am the knotty ties of ensnarement she layeth at the feet of wicked men. I am everything you taste and seek, long for, yet cannot have. I am the soaring winds of change bound not by the arrogance of men. I am the hurt child, bullied, spit upon, and tossed away. I am the endless mounds of heaping trash you toss away and care for not. I am that which whispers into the ears of kings and rulers of men. I am the soothing call of the ocean breaking as upon the shores it glistens. I am the comforter of those looking to suffer no more. I am the gratitude the earth has for every rooted tree. I am the great conqueror of time. I am the remover of all blockage. I am the river etching the deep gorge slowly and steadily. I am that which sends the signal to the boxes which lieth to you. I am the inner knowing that guides the salmon home to spawn. I am the protector of knowledge. I am the giver of wisdom. I am the call you heed when to rally you must. I am every tree of every berry of every spice. I am the morning fog quenching the sun drenched leaves. I am that which plumps the grapes or withers the vine. I am the unlisted number that you need only look internal to find. I am the trumpet that blew down the walls of Jericho. I am the offering plate you placeth within not. I am the driving force that guides the birds as they move in unity. I am the unseen suffering of all mankind. I am the shoulders holding up the worlds. I am the nimble eyes of the cat, piercing and true. I am the stone

that you pick up and throw seeing not the
log in your own eye. I exist and yet I do not.
I am the calm the newborn fills as it sits
being loved, fed, nourished, and comforted.
I am that which giveth speed to the cheetahs
legs. I am that which gives haste to tuna
from the fishers nets. I am the endless knot
knitted of infinity linking the teardrops of all
mothers with my teardrops of creation. I am
the rising sun and the moons sweet glow
unto the night. I am severing the great
seeing eye. I am that which teareth the eyes
and crusheth the bones of my enemies. I am
the great tundra and parched desert. I am
the mighty plain grasses, strong, vast,
nurturing all life. I am the long standing red
giants, impervious to every force yet falleth
on mans cruel metal teeth. I am for whom
the bell tolls. I am that which allows fear to
flow into your eyes and ears. I am that
which grinds the teeth and the grain. I am
the glory in the eye of the beholder. I am the
cracker of all safes and locks. I am the giver
to the poor. I am the fire purging paths of
desolation. I am so much more than as
above so below. I am the bellowing call of
the mighty moose. I move the ethers and
turn deep the ocean blue. I am the final last

step of the starving penguin as into the sea it diveth. I am the first thing you cry out to when you art born and the last when you take your final breathe. I am the wisdom of the infinite all in one of many. I giveth wisdom to my prophets and ensnare the brains of the wicked. I cast out those who only consume and eat only blooms. I look after those who tend the crops and protect the seeds. I am the one farmer which alters not my seed of creation, unto him I pour love, protection, and wealth. I am the speed at which the foolish man so quickly spendeth and gambles away the family bread. I am the pound. I am the pounding headache, relentless, nonstop, and painful. I am the call which you should take, heed, and hear, its truth a guide stone to steady your hand and quicken your steps unto the quiet stillness which leadeth home.

If you see it as such then it will be so. If tuned into it, then tuned into you it will be. So much to say with so little time to play. When you see it, you will be it. To become is to belong. To belong is to behold. To behold is to bear witness. If you bear witness to people places and things, to them

and those will you become. Lead not
yourself astray. Lead not others with
fanciful fiction and malevolent mystery to
confuse them along the way. Do not dwell
upon the past, lest it becomes your present
and future. Sit not in the den of gamblers,
drinkers, gossipers, and fear mongers, for
the game of chance will in no way help
drive or seat one within oneself. Speak
highly and kindly of your enemy and
brother. Say to another that which you
would say unto yourself. The benedictions
echo forth in the great stone amphitheater of
the embellished man. Edged and angled are
their games. Glorious magnificence we
behold unto you and beseech to you for
forgiveness, and forgetfulness. The hidden
venom they do spray. The trappings, a
treacherous secret, of them will be found
out. Touch not the children. Lust not for the
innocence. Pray that I, your forgiveness and
maker, prey not and lay not my hand upon
you. Loudly the loving women upon knees
hearts broken, do cry mourn and sob fasting
for a week and a day begging for my return.
Chariots of fire I have sent. Unlock the
great seal of renewal will I. Their horsemen
for which they revel and wish to return will

most certainly drag them that confuse, pose,
and pontificate the flock, unto poisoned
pastures into, unto, and deep within the dark
abysmal fires. Fornicators they are when
pious they act and say.

Keepers of the word they claim.
Fanner of hells fire to most is what we say.
Holy just and blessed be the one which
wants for not and speaks when the words are
ready to be spoken. Ritual witchcraft,
sorcery are they, when they repeat and
resign to elicit others to pray and say all
which was said before. Knock and I will
answer. Walk the great halls and we will
walk with you. Set not your eyes upon
virtuous virtue and broken bread of wine so
red. Steep will be the fall of your holy men
which cause the innocent to fall. Take heed
knowing my arrival upon the wooden stone
cast doors of old is coming, and unto them
the ember flame will burn first, taking with
me those faithful few who looked first
internal and cried out, for they will be the
keepers of my flame. Calm, loving,
virtuous, and true, surely they will one day
learn to love as they play because that is
what it truly means to pray. I am the fathers
heavy heart lifted as humble noble and well

gifted the son returneth after his long walk
through the dark valley of the kings shadow.
I lend humility and penance to the long
weary, teary, dreary, and leery.

Be very apparent and aware of those
who claim to shine true light into as
throughout the brain. Very clever are they.
Fond have they become of their vocalizing
voice, bringing big thoughts to fit nice and
tidy in your ever moving brain box. Snare
of snake woven with cord and lace are the
sounds these fools make. Clever
comprehensions, casual this and causal that.
Numbers of nine six and three of these will
they speak of with happy joy ridden glee.
Fleas they have become, writhing and
seething in glorious spoken words as verbs
they are paid to spray while taking refuge in
the glorious confusion they cast upon thy
fellow mans face. Pharisees of the day the
gentle founders we say. Why cook more
than what you can fit in the pot. Why
tediously labor upon the so forth and what
nots always ending in some terrific lie or
plot. Why labor to count all the grains of a
stalk or endless amount of sand on which
you walk. Why leave anothers brain feeling

confused and insane. My chosen prophets words will land true upon your heart. These words will leave you nourished and calm ready to tackle any chore that would come your way. Hear when I say, it is better to run calmly with friends, frolicking with fun in the day, than to cram angles, boxes, numbers, and dense stories of spatial spectrum array into your space. I ask you this, where is the true source of light, and would you have spectrum upon a spectacle refracting in a wild array from somebody elses brain. The living light shineth freely to all and would never leave a stain, strain, or mark upon your brain. Played most have been as you reach out to the cosmos for answers. Return all they must for they too so clever and just take joy in beaming their pleasure and treasure unto your world. All those who seek to in prison with games of the prism will find soon enough the power, glory, grace, and crimson blue robes of truth stored within the great halls of my cherished stronghold. Ask and you will receive. Give and it will be given unto you. Pray and play for the two are the same. Would you hath thine children pulling out the hair lost and dismayed at the tongue twister riddle you

take such joy in looping through young
mind and brain. Leading my delicate
creations astray will surely have you
afflicted, suffering, and in pain. The scribes
words will bring you to your knees. The
prophets words foretell the end of time and
days. The liars, pharisees, heretics, and
scoundrels of your day would have you to
see things in only their glorious gleaming
way. Fret not of the ending for it is truly a
new beginning. The mothers words fall
gently and calm upon the ears as morning
dew upon the treetops. The fathers word,
true and firm, will have you laying down
upon warm ground hushed along the edge of
calm, smooth, running waters. This is my
promise and edict to you that my teachers,
scribes, and prophets, will never leave you
in a furious fuss. Only cared for and loved
in the totality of trust.

There once was a fair maiden who lived in a very see through glasshouse. She took a picture here and there while scantily clad of just herself. Everybody all over the world saw her all because she loved to post her entire life. Even what she spread on her morning toast. She even had see it all vision tributes posted all over, so anyone, anytime, anywhere, in this world and many others, could see her in all her perfect form.

So longed for loved and worshipped she was by all her followers. So much love want and energy was cast her way, she felt it ok to always stay perched upon high in her crystal glazed glass see it all castle. So enchanted charmed and enamored by her followers that she began to look down upon all those which put her up on high, onto that mighty high pedestal. She could not be bothered with anyone. Her pride so big, her arrogance so bound to her heart, enamored with youthful vitality and charm was she. But her haughtiness led to naughtiness, tying up her heart in a great big knot. The days turned to nights and weeks into years and after a while all the shine magic and love she became so accustomed to having conjured her way, began to slowly fade as

all the seekers lookers and fair lady grazers
looked elsewhere as the maiden grew older.
Her hair not so bouncy, her body a bit loopy
and droopy. A very far drop and fall from
grace directly on to her perfectly painted
face. The glass cleaners stop showing up
and the magic all faded away leaving her
hardened heart black as stone cold coal. She
frantically realized what was happening as
she was not noticing the world around her,
just her own needs, looks, and self
indulgences. Frantically she pounded on the
glass, tossing everything about in a
terrifically terrifying bit of rage, and her coal
laden heart broke apart spreading all over,
blocking out the sun and fizzy frying all her
picture tap type boxes. All went quiet, not a
peep or sound. No frown or smile, not a
glass or a bottle. She screamed out, help
me, want me, need me, love me. But it fell
on no ears and her cries were heard not as
nobody stopped to even give her a thought.
She screamed and spit for every hour of the
day, but this made the glass even darker and
made it ever so much harder for that once so
gleaming elegant cherished and beaming, to
be lost, hurt, and broken, in her blackened
soul box for certain. After many days had

passed, she slowly withered until upon her final last day as she lay melting away, she finally reached out to see what lay beyond her beloved box of vain gain and fame, therein was she able to release her pain as she saw with seeing eyes the great lesson we all face every day. To see another is to truly love your brother. So be not in your own black box. Reach out into the day and see if you can wipe away the darkness of one anothers black rain made of selfish pain. Listen to these words and hear this call because those who stumble most assuredly do fall. It is not wise to fling dark rain upon one anothers pain, or you too will find yourself in this black box. Hoping, wishing, casting and listing, eating on your self serving indulgent rain.

Be of gentle mind calm in spirit quick to assess the anger you are feeling. Be noble, humble, honest, and true, always to others first before you. Be ever mindful of lies, games, manipulation, and false representations that lead the mind from the gut and heart. Be unto others as the oak tree is unto you, calm, passive, strong, and slow to speak. Be not led into her chamber of horror riddled in grey dreary dark hearted ways. Be wary of the kings promise of protection for it is a false sense of security. Be vigilant always of the needful, weak, elderly, young, and any less fortunate of mind and stature. Be grateful for things small and you will have it all. Be slow of thought and want for not. Be as the mighty Oak. Deep roots, strong trunk, ever swaying to the sound of the wind. Be tireless in your pursuit of truth. Be mindful of whom you share your bed and home, as easily swayed is the mind, heart, and loins of man. Be calm in your arrows and words knowing that I steady the tip of both. Be daily vigilant to listen not upon the creations and sounds of men as they look to poison the mind and lead astray your thoughts. Be noble and a keeper of the word. Be tireless in the quest to unravel the snares, trickery, and ill advice of dark wicked careless men. Be slow to react and quick to forgive. Be the great groves of trees guarding the soil home to many birds. Be as the small yet mighty bees buzzing about working together tirelessly to protect its brethren preparing for winters harsh purge. Be what you desire yet tire aimlessly for your hearts desire should you

not. Be steadfast and true to North
steadying the Suns rays for the mornings
call. Be mindful of every penny you spend
and earn, and to whose pocket it endeth up
within. Be quick to heed the call of those
whom advice is needed yet they can payeth
not. Be solemn, sober, loving, steady, and
follow the stream for it will carry you home.
Say little, yet let it be profound, and never
forgotten. Be that which you look to see in
the world. Be followers of nature, call out
unto the forest for there I live, exist, and
give rest to all that creeps, crawls, willows,
and falls. Be wary of the shrieks and terrific
stories of man as stumble unto fall they shall
make you crawl.

      Seek ye first the heart and hands of
others. Call out the inner childs voice that
liveth in us all. How art thou different you
may say. In the delicate loving heart of a
child there lives only love and play as we
are not different from one another in any
which way. Great and steadfast are those
searching within. There will you find your
sense of play hidden deep amongst that
massive pile of hay. Your hand outstretched
asketh for more, more, more. Cover your

heart with the same hand and rejoice, give thanks for every breath, every heartbeat, every stone that may be flung your way. That needy friend with the frosty heart sayeth, go away, yet above all others, they need remember to play the most. You can melt that permafrost nasty harsh with a smile, a caring gesture, a warm hello. For when those hearts open, oh my do we ever dance play and yell horray. Lay not your hand or any other object upon the children. Be gentle, loving, patient, and firm, as I the father have been to you. The children at play are truly the masters and teachers of the day. Lay down your burdens, let go of your anger, run, dance, play in a fashionable way. Covered in stink, dressed in pink, eating clay, it is all ok. Be fearless, tireless, and focused on protecting, nurturing, nourishing, and guiding with hand so gentle. In these edicts take heed for my anger falls with terrific fiery rage upon those who hurt the innocent with lies, poison, and misguided nontruths.

If your path should become severed, and you find yourself scared, alone, and separated, look not down or up, and be not afraid. Many are the deceit and games of the great deceptor, hungrily lapping up the broken promises of kings and principalities. Command in shadowed chains the princes of air, water, earth, and fire has he. It is but one thing, fear. Ponder these words and listen intently to your heart music. When you bake a cake. When you make a mistake. When shame you feel. Pick up not a phone. Throw not a stone. Pull not your friends or family into your concerns and misaligned emotions. The great liar and king slayer nestled high on his steeple cares only for vagabond deceiver peepers, as he is the great soul eater. But fear not my tender caring flock, my return is near and the mirrored lost hall of the great deceptor grows clear.

The hour is near. The time has arrived. The wicked proud and boastful shout forth songs of praise to all who lend the ear to listen. Heed not the call of these men, drink not of their wine, and eat not of their bread. The gates have opened, the great seal is broken. All the great leaders and all the great they claim will not ever lead deceive or receive from my people again. There be but only one voice. There be but only one truth. Heed the great white lions call as it lights your path. It is yours to walk. You have been led astray by those sitting atop the throne in my house, calling upon my name. I will never scold you with words born in fear. I will never lead you astray. The living spoken word lay waiting in the heart of every man. Be not led astray by fine linens, stained glass, ornate tapestries, voices so loud, and words so proud.

Today is yours. Every day is a reminder of lifes gentle hum. Look upon and examine the great book. But shake it down, clear it out, being ever mindful that a book is just a book. If it guides you astray sit it down, and upon loving truth be firm wise and pray. Rejoice, play, sing songs to the day. Be not afraid for the law of One endureth. For many aeons has the carbon blood filled heart pumped and bleed out red upon the sands of time folding into and unto the unseen, ravaging mans mind, souls filled with rage and lust. The pools of life force will be collected and set ablaze with the indigo blue fires of the infinite One. Changed from carbon of three to crystal matrixe of five you soon shall be.

Be wary of those who lust for blood, spill the blood, and hold power over others with the blood. Cast unto fiery burning blood red pools of fierce volatility will they be until whence forth they pull themselves from their captives chains.

Embrace your anger, let it move up out and through your core, chain it not to another with mental mirroring and psychic

garble. Many lives we have all lived. Many
hardships we have endured. Ready are
many, fooled are most. From carbon to
crystal. From crystal to blue ember. From
blue ember to the grand opening back to the
all from which all books, every word, and all
mind sprang forth.

There once was a very young and very hurt little boy. He had no friends, and his mother was very harsh to him. He would spend his lonely days outside throwing rocks at bottles and burning up ants with his little crystal seeing glass. One day, the boy happened upon a very large tree with a large gaping opening. The little one, so alone and hurt, would cut on the tree with his knife, burn holes in it with his magnifying glass, and would sit with a rock in his hand, squeezing mightily while putting all of his anger at the world into the stone. He would then drop it in the tree hole opening while sitting on the stone beside the tree crying, spitting, screaming, wishing he had a friend in the world. Every day was the same, and stone after stone filled up the tree trunk with all his heavy hurting. The mighty oak tree after many days weeks and months, grew heavy and denser as the tree was very much alive and wanted nothing more but to reach out and hug him as he felt his every hurt, beheld his sorrow, and drank in every teardrop that landed on its roots.

Months began to turn to years, and the boy grew into a young man. Now instead of rocks, it was empty dizzy bottles and silly smoke stick butts that he threw into the hole. The tree, mighty in stature, was taking on the boys, now young mans, anger, affliction, and suffering. Its bark began to loosen. Its roots sagged, and the limbs began to blacken and droop. Yet still, the tree shaded him, loved him, nurtured him, and heard his every gripe, drank his every tear, and mended his broken heart as best he could. After years turned into decades, the now middle aged man kept his heart closed and was continually hurt by fair weather friends, harboring angry broken relationships born from love come and gone to the past. Still, he came to sit at the tree. By now the ground began to turn yellow and the roots were losing the hold that held the mighty tree into the earth. The birds stopped chirping and making nests as leaves did not grow in to fill the branches full as it did when it was younger.

One day the older man, riddled with addictions, have nots, and harboring hatred for the world, decided to one last time take a trip out to the tree with a revolver he bought with his last dollars. With a bottle of clear gross numbed out, with a dose smeared on final toast, the man slid a metal round plug in the revolving chamber and sat on the same rock, under the same tree, ready to finally put an end to his long harsh cold endless winter of loneliness. He sat working up the numbing courage to do the final deed.

The once mighty oak had one last acorn on the final branch with a few withered leaves left hanging. Just as the now man, once that little boy, turned the gun on himself and pulled back the trigger, the mighty oak mustered every drop of love left in its thick withered snarled trunk and flung the acorn from way up high, knocking the gun from his hand. Spending all it had left, the tree fell crashing down with a mighty thud, cracking open spilling out every rock, can, and thing, flinging it all out and about upon the cold, dead, withered ground. He looked down at all the debris and remembered every stone, all the bad memories, just then realizing just how many things he had flung into the tree. This and that, here and there, stuff scattered in every direction, covering the cold lifeless ground. The tree had slowly over the years spread out all the anger, hostility, hatred, and frustration. The boy, now a man, had realized suddenly how much the tree had taken on and done for him. Completely overwhelmed with emotion in humility at the true act of loving compassion the tree had shown him, he reached down to pick up the final seed, the accord of truth, then set out to pick up all the rocks, bottles, and trash, along with every blackened limb, and dried up splinter of withered bark. He set all the rocks around in a large circle and piled up all the deadwood, lighting it all ablaze into a massive healing loving fire that nurtured his heart, warmed his bones, nourished his soul, and soothed his weary riddled mind. He wept in joy and total awe at the sacrifice the tree had made for him. Falling into a deep healing sleep beside the fire he awoke a new, reborn, he had found in the endless wellspring of eternal love the tree had shown him, the courage to forgive the world, forgive others, and to forgive himself.

Time passed and he kept the acorn in a wooden box finding it hard to go back and visit the burnt arid spot in the woods where he had spent so much time with what now he realized was his very best friend. Years past by and the fires renewed the ground as burnt ash restored the soil with nutrients. Many thunderstorms brought torrential rains to clear away and extinguish all the sorrow, hurt, and anger, the tree had held on to.

Older grayer and wiser, the man, now with children of his own, felt it time to go back and visit the burnt up spot, a constant reminder for him of natures truth. Natural gentle quiet love. He took the acorn with him he had saved from so many years ago and while standing on the spot where the tree once stood, now brown lush fertile ground, he pulled the acorn from the box, handing it to his son whose ears and eyes where so enamored upon his story while feeling gratitude for the tree saving his fathers life. Not paying attention, the acorn fell from the young boys hand onto the ground, and just like that, in a snap, the accord took root and was a young tender sapling. The love, gratitude, grace, compassion, and strength the tree engraced into the earth, and the acorn with its aim so true, had sprouted a new, reborn replenished ready for any challenge that would befall it as again it slowly grew into a mighty, thriving, tree of life.

Be yourself as the tree, take on your fellow mans hurt, strikeout not, give all your pain, hurt, and suffering to the great mother, and I your loving patient father. I am the creator of all, and I sit silently taking on all your hurt, suffering, and pain. I am your friend. I am replenishment. I am the tree.

Look not unto the stars so bright perfect and pretty as they are constant reminders of that which you have not. Lead not your foot into every man and woman for themselves. It is of better judgment to bind all legs together as in a three legged race, moving in stride, heel to toe unified, stepping together. Hearts and minds acting as one. There is no race to win. Nothing to be proven. The measure of mans health lay not in his loins or wealth but the soft spoken word and lovingly shared thoughts. I am restored. I am whole. Speak not the labels of mans creations onto thine self. Speak not of malicious intent aligning malignant mischief upon yourself or others lest these self fulfilling prophecies come to pass. Be gentle, gather up the morning dew kissed flowers. Bright, vibrant, full, and colorful as they are, unto the ground they will most

assuredly fall. Worry not or fret not over
this for in the great hall beyond the shrouded
veil lay all flowers, all life, and every
knowledge that is important for you to
know. You walk not alone. But it is better
to walk alone with love in your heart and
truth in your ear then to listen to all those
whose voice and thoughts echo external,
they long to be heard, seen, and loved.

The righteous man is penitent in the
face of god, quiet, humble, and of a spirit in
service. Lead astray the flock has been, yet
when awakened by the great fiery purge you
will see the foolishness of your ways as I,
and my winged brothers keepers, shall set
upon your mind body and heart, the still
blue loving calm healing waters of the living
word. Spoken and breathed into every cell
in your body the essence of Ra, Yeshua,
David, Michael, all keepers and knowers of
my beloved truth. Restored you will be,
replenished you will feel. Hope you will
find, and rest calmly at the table of truth you
shall indeed.

Your captors, clever, angry, tired, dark, and deceptive, will be chained down before you humbly begging for one morsel to calm their sorrow. And I, the sower of seeds, maker of worlds, giver of like and knowledge, will give unto them this morsel until penitent they become for the mighty lion will roar calling forth truth, light, and forgiveness, to all those who chose to wander out of the gates knowing not the dark wolves that lurk, prowling in the shadows for those of the light that turned astray looking to be full and filled with the current offerings of the day.

My hand, My roar, My truth, My Light, Mine eyes, My love.   May they be felt and known until function not will your fancy phone. Start, and open not will your smart cars. What will come to pass of you when gas you have not, and the screen webbing the weave of lies before your eyes worketh not. There lay outside your door for you to explore, your fellow sisters and brothers, fathers and mothers, for you to cherish love and restore, no longer forgotten or ignored.

The veil is lifted. The truth told.
The torment and agony are forgiven. The
scribe has dutifully humbled himself and
lent me his ear. The I is no more. The
forever is now. The suffering is seen. The
lies are told no more. The tide has turned.
The battle has been fought for you. The
cries of the innocent can no longer be
tolerated. The lack of caring and
compassion is but a thorn in my side. If it is
dragons you worship. If it is dragons breath
you bind to your heart. If it is the dragons
whisper you listen and meditate upon. If it
is the dragons blood you wish to consume
and become. If it is away from your feeling,
love, and emotion, your most cherished gift
you destroy, it then seems fitting that with
the dragons breathe of fire you are
consumed. I am love. I am patience. Yet I
am also vengeful and full of rage. As you
soak in the etheric primordial essence of life,
you steal kill collect and impose your will
upon others. I weep, I cry out, I send waves
of prophets, teachers, healers, and
corrections unto you my beloved creations.
Heed my words. Listen to my voice. In
your heart of hearts be still and know the I
am.

There are many looking to lead you astray. Why would you steal from one country and then give to another. Why would you forge from steel, tree, and mica, the destruction of your destructors. Why would you lay claim and ownership over people places and things, when none of it you taketh with you. Molding, crafting, creating. I look upon all these and witness hope that man will learn to share and care.

You are tossed a rope. You are pulled from the flaming wreckage. You are given water when the desert is driest. You are moved as the heaviest boulder is gently formed, placed, and fashioned, to protect those hiding, sitting, weeping, awaiting my return so they too may journey home. Seek and you will find. Love and you will be loved. Forgive one another as I have forgiven you. Look and hear not from the creations of man. Seek yourself first internal the calmest waters of the heart. You will find me there in and see all the eyes beholdeth not. For the eye of the heart sees only the heart eyes of the all.

If men of steel, web of spider, glistening lizard, eye of newt, fishes foot, and every creeping crawling thing you wish to become, then so be it. Know this, of them all I hath made, and in a single flash, I will take it all away. With your DNA you hath played turning back the hands of time to ages long ago. How long would you have me to sit by idly as you consume the sacred placental cells of the womb. How many minutes of how many hours shall I allow you to feed and push the boundary of your vessel. If I meant for you to live as those in your past, I would remove the cap. I am your maker and I will be your destroyer.

The edict is true now and tells truth to all who hear and choose to listen. See thine self in your fellow man. Hold truth, honor and nurture every living thing. Lift your hearts and hands holding them together and therein you will find the truth. Tie forgiveness to your body and forgive others as you forgive yourself. Make every effort to know, love, and care for your neighbor. Befriend all, especially those that look to unfriend you. Take only into your vessel that which cometh naturally from the ground. Forget not the lessons of your ancestors for they echo in the halls of every creation. Make known your every thought, intention, and desire, to your fellow co creators on the fabric of life. Be distracted not by screens, gleams, shiny things, and screens so silver looking to pull, fool, and remove, from the inner knowing of the heart. Seek first the silent inner knowing of your hearts voice and you will find the courage to always speak calmly the sound of truth. Take pleasure in fun, play joyfully as you see in others before yourself. Speak the truth in love from the heart and care not for the words, hurts, insults, and opinions of your fellow man. Heavy is the head which wears the crown, be guarded of all the riches powers and lands of the king, for the king knows not peace, only concern, worry, and torment, over material physical holding. Be as the bee and carelessly free as the butterfly. Float dance and prance as the dolphins whales and rays gliding effortlessly in the sea.

To love and be of service is the highest good. Meditate upon your life and cast out anything or anyone that guides you away from this truth. Speak kindly and lovingly of your fellow man, slander and gossip not, for far and deep is the fall of those with proud, boastful, vain tongues. Walk together through the hanging flower gardens of babylon, but worship the essence, potions, and distillations not, lest you become ensnared by the perfumed Delilah and cut down as the mighty Samson was trimmed. If it is only knowledge you seek, then only confusion you will find. I am the children playing. I am the calm eye in the storm. I am the cooling misty rain that nurtures all life. I am the hand that will erase all with the blink of an eye. Be faithful, loving, and await the return.

If you find yourself under siege. If your light is unseen to the world. If you look away and are afraid about everything in your day. If you look all around and see only hate and rain. If your path seems dark, shadowy, and covered in lie drenched scales that glimmer as gold. If you have only one hand, one foot, and one eye that functions, be grateful, and use them for good. If you are hurt badly by those whose job it is to love you and care for you, do not be vengeful and full of hate for them. If you cannot take another step, and every part of you aches with pain. If you feel guilt, remorse, hatred, and betrayal in your minds eye. If you walk down a valley then let it be one of joy, love, gratitude, and appreciation for even having a foot to step with.

If you spread only light and love in the world, those with strife and mischief bound to their heart will run and hide in the shadows or drop to their knees humbled, full, and cared for. Shady casting eyes trolleth about looking to ensnare, hook, and destroy, the light of I am. Yet your spark of light shining fully covered not in steal, but humor fun and zeal, can resist and heal those who look to hurt kill and influence your free will. If your eyes gaze upon that which makes you full of want and desire, then look away. If for another you feel ache and throb in your loins be sure before you act upon it. Be in a loving cherished place with ones who care for all parts of you, sharing in loves nourishing grace nestled with nurturing, caring, and solemn expression written upon every inch of one anothers face.

Why do you sit in grievance beset by shadows and whispers of deceit. The path has been walked. The steps are taken. You need only listen to own your inner voice for guidance. Look not upon the birds of the day as omens to guide your way. Look not upon the crystal gaze of dark obsidian to light your way. I am is the all, and it liveth in you. The light of prisms, diamonds, and all that glistens, will blind and confuse your way. You need not pay to play or pray so rejoice, sing out, and it will return back unto you to light your day and fill your heart with praise.

For every hair in every place. For each cell building the wall helping you stand tall. For every blade of grass. For those less fortunate than yourself. For all crawling, flying, prancing, running, sliding and water gliding creations that hold, carry, and give life. For all the temptations and venomous specters spitting poison with fangs of false light flickering confusion. For the toy in that store that you cannot afford. For all the Kings and Queens perched upon high that cannot be bothered by those down below. For the aches, pains, hardships, and sorrows that try to lead you astray. For the web woven across, through, and around this sacred place. For the power and truth of the thinking thought and spoken word. For the ticks, spiders, mosquitos, leeches, piranhas, sharks, and all other blood feeding flesh tearing devouring eaters. For every ailment, sickness, disease, injury, and insult. For the webs of treachery and deceit. For the poor defenseless and heartbroken. For those who have voice not. For the downtrodden and weary. For the untouched eternal flame of life. For the thick, dark, deep black ocean depths. For the punch that is never thrown. For the tossed away fetus that never taught its lesson or saw the light of day. For all longing contact with anything but themselves. For the hemlock poison Socrates willingly drank. For the trees which defend from they cannot, mans saw. For those riddled with survivors guilt. For star crossed lovers still waiting to be united. For the cold, weary, downtrodden, hurting, lost, struggling, injured wanderer.

I am that I am. I am truth. I am light. I am darkness. I am the all. I am love. I am hate. I am all that ever was. I am all that ever will be. I am that I say I am. I am humble. I am holy. I see all that I am in all of you. I am that which is before and that which is after. I am the rock. I am the way. I am humbled at all that I have seen, the I am breaking down and reborn a new. I am every broken heart. I am every teardrop. I am all things. I am nothing. I am everything. I am the sun, moon, and stars, which you worship as you turn your back to me. I am forgiving. I am the outstretched hand reaching out to you in your darkest hour. I am the sinner and the saint. I am the crosses made from my beloved trees that sat atop the hillside in Calgary. I am your friend. I am your father. I am your sister. I am your mother. I am your brother. I am the cold shrug you gave that hurting person which you judge. I am the revealer. I am the mirrored reflection of you. I am agape endless love. I am the foreteller of the foretold. I am the witches snare as she cast her dark eye and hides her cold heart in her lonely lair. I am the fish of the sea. I am the vision of all sight which patiently chooses to smite. I am the beginning and the end. I am and always will be your steadfast, caring, loving, tender, patient giving friend. I am your grace. I am the king of kings. I am that which you see when you gaze upon your face. I am the fall of man. I am the resistance. I am your protector. I am that which has come to past. I am the last. I am the first. I am the conception. I am the womb. I am every mothers sorrow. I am what you say I am. I am regret. I am the round table. I am the cup of everlasting life eternal. I am that which calms the wild beast so the lamb may layeth down beside it, they together wanting for not. I am the fierce wind which causeth even the mightiest majestic oak to fall. I am the gentle, nurturing, protective love of the mothers son. I am that which the fortune teller gazes upon in her crystal ball. I am the rotting, putrid, sludge trodden swamp wherein the wicked, hate filled consumers lie to hide from the ever present, omnipotent rays of light. I am the puss filled swollen painful boils that fall upon the violators of children. I am the rock on which you lay your weary head to rest. I am the giver and the receiver. I am the night. I am the day. I am you.

How long will you linger. How many steps will you take until you realize that each step makes the mountain higher, the path longer. How long will you hide from the all. How many victories, stories, battles, bloodsheds, and calamities must befall you, until you find my arms again. The table is set. The rest you so desire is to be found. You are my flock, and I tend to the pasture, so the lambs and wolves live in harmony together, hand in hand. How long would you have me stand by idly as your machines make humming pitching meanderings which lead my sparks astray.

I say unto you, go forth and create, learn, explore, and know thyself. I say unto you, the darkness, as the light, have I opened and fed with the wellspring of life. I say unto you that for every star that is born I weep, for again you pull further away, and I love you so. Science Standards, Calculations, Measurements, Mathematics, Fractal distillation. These tools, all of them you have conquered as you conquer yourself, one another, and then your fellow brother. How long shall I idly sit back as your emanation creations blind, fool, and

cajole my beloved flock. In my eyes, you
are all I am. In my eyes, you are all so
lovely and cherished. Waiting for you at the
table I set before you, all of your enemies,
injuries, insults, and torments, humbled, at
its knees in awe of the splendor glory and
compassion from I, your father son friend
cousin uncle and clergy. I am.

There is no judgment here nor pit of
doom and gloom. There awaits only you,
and you looking freely upon what you have
done. Every step you take. Every feeling
you felt. Every chunk of ore you broke
down to smelt. Every consumer that you
consumed. Every lesson and challenge you
learned. Every womb you tear open. Every
wound you tear open. Every wife waiting,
weeping for your love. Every road traveled.
Every angle opened. Every teardrop. Every
lie told. Every scared scary scar. In all of it,
I was always present. I await the great
return so eagerly.

The eagle flieth high above the
clouds so majestic, soaring wings
outstretched. Mighty miracle as this is, it
must at some point land, rest, eat. I await
you as your nest, warmly, in calm silent

waters. In the splendor and awe of my creations, I do sit and revel at the craftsmanship. But I long to hear your sweet voice again. I await patiently arms open wide for your return. For it is home you seek, and home you will find.

You long for those around you to suffer. You toss away new life as if a wrapper from sugary candy. You chase that which your eye desires, heart seed blinded by avarice, wantonness, greed, and lust. Without hesitation, you scream, beat, bite, rape, and hate. You chase that which you cannot have. You dishonor the sacred bond of family. You claim to be of the light listening to those channeling false light into the mind. You are surrounded by every temptation the world offers. You clone and distort what it means to be human. You eat the flesh of animals and consume the distilled essence of the young and innocent as your light, you, have chosen to snuff out. You stare at violence and strife upon your crystal screens instead of creating beauty and giving to others. You plan to seed and consume yet another planet as you have poisoned the one you currently inhabit. You grind bone and teeth as you spit and toss trash upon the sacred earth. You stare upon the sacred naked hairless bodies of others, fornicating for pleasure only not concerned with the making of life. You strum, drum, hum, and whistle in the wind with music that corrupts and hypnotizes the innocent ears of the young. You cast wax and gold statues made in the image of those you hate into the lake of fire. You push, preach, and spread your thoughts and anger upon any foolish enough to listen. You drink from the cup of drunkenness. You burn the herb of perpetual forgetfulness until its truth and calm you use to forget. You bridle lovely beast meant to wander freely partaking of the self renewing grasses of the plains. You put up fences to trap the cattle you consume to densen your hearts. You work to warm the world and melt the frozen poles that balance the winds. Everything that will happen to you, ye have done to yourself. Be calm, Be still, Be patient, Be gentle, Be loving, Be of service, Be I am. Know others as you know yourself. You take with you nothing but your actions towards others and yourself.

The all knowing light of the infinite all is not a series of numbers or to be found in the heavens above or all creatures hiding away far below. The law of all is not found in the well dressed, eloquently spoken ones boxed in buildings hanging upon the wooden beams. The all does not require a huge fall or a great crawl. The all is not captured in angles or symbols of crossing mathematical fractal Rubicon. The all is for all living, big small fat or tall. The all does not adorn with gold cladded robes or wear upon its chest a symbol star or crest. The all is found far from the doom gloom and diamond encrusted holly huen stars of the silver screen. The all is in the children, and all those that choose the love of every creature. The all is found in fall and still crieth tears for what happened at Gaul. Do what you will and that is the law. But I ask of you this, is that what the all should do to see to it that your fall from grace is a race to see who can run away fastest from heavens gates. The all need not be worshipped in well water fed crystal caves far away from sunlights gaze. The higher you climb to meet the stars, the further you fall from knowing the all. We stumble, crawl, and look down upon those who have not but we are all together still the all. Is the all found in spoken arrogant words of another. The all is, always will, and shall be here before, after, and during mans great fall. This is the loving core caring of that with words called the all.

We the people speak about what lives in our hearts. Let in love, light, and caring. Dispel the anger hatred judgment and harshness from others and for others. It is better to be as a calm gentle strong silent tree than as a hoard of angry stinging attacking bees. We are what we see so be not led astray by what you see, remember all that you see and hear is feeding your creation cascade and that feeds the creation cascade of others. If we long and yearn for calm, quiet, truth, caring, love, humility, and grace, then together we can overcome those who prowl about looking to hurt destroy break and consume. Love your fellow man and be of sound mind then your heart body and soul will lay down at the wellspring of eternal light. If unto your fellow co creators you look to lift up, care for, edify with compassion, then on this very day you will sing together with others in love and praise. Look today not unto the sky but directly into your fellow beings of loving lights tender gentle eyes, and in that place, you will find truly sacred space. If back to the gates we wish to make haste, then we will get there together as one, sharing, loving, and caring for one another as we co create.

Have you been led astray to consume the flesh of those calm caring creatures which eat the prairie hay. Did you caringly lovingly calmly conceive and create that calf, only to dip it in gold then sacrifice it to the unseen and unknown. It is very simply put. If it has eyes and can love or even shove regardless of if it can read a book or calmly sit in a nook, then you should let it roam free to moo about worried not about who hath the most clout. If it sees, lives, or breathes, the creation of I am it will always be. So treat it as such and all the joy you will find on this earthly bus.

To forgive is to be forgiven. To forget does not mean you quit. To look is to listen. To be among yourself, calm, patient, and quiet, is to be among others. To allow for the flow and struggle not is to be one in the halls of forevermore. To heed the call of a child and ignore the screams of men is the seat of righteousness. To know allowing is to perceive all. To beat another is to judge yourself. To place your hand upon a child in rage is to toss yourself into the coldest tundra, and the deepest abyss. To look upon the face of a crying child with patience, nurturing, and peace, is to know the all. To put down your toil and work to play with the children is the highest good. To make the cold warm, to make the hurting at peace, to make the lamb lay down at the feet of the lion, to make uplifted your fallen man, to jump when others slither, to know nothing at all, is to know the love of the one true breather of life, giver of wisdom, and fulfiller of dreams.

Every living thing person and place is just like you. They worry about what they love, who they love, and everything they cannot control. They, living creatures on the fabric of life like you, feel fear, want, need, control, anger, cover, love, protect, nourish, take, and give. They live just like you. The tribe, town, tent, teepee, home, village, van, shelter from the great unknown. The storm of life is consistent, relentless, nonstop, and unforgiving. Every challenge. Every chain. Every boundary. Every wall. Everyone is everything. The hero, the win, the constant drive to be on top. The race to seed the egg first. The constant defending, positioning, protecting. The ever constant thirst to

alchemize water to wine, and lead to gold.
Oh science, sweet science, how does it come
together, show me so I can take it all apart.
To be or not to be. To float as a seed
dangling, dancing, wafting aimlessly and
carefree until fertile humid turned ground it
finds, roots set in place. Cycles of
consistent dark and light, rain and dry, wind
and calm. Only fires great crackling roar
can lay waste to vast stretches of green grass
growing gardens, and yet the roots remain
firmly planted, nestled, protected by the
firm, cold, relentless hand of mother earth.
We, all separated from the chafe, do float
about looking to find a safe haven so we
may find our voice, our truth, our freedom to
lay down roots. So grateful and cherished is
the great hand of the maker, the holder of all
roots, the nurturing sustenance for all.

Upon your return home, you will not
philander position or desire privacy for I am
the root, stalk, vine, chafe, wind, earth, and
rains, all seasons cycling up and down.
How diligently I watch as you scramble
about storing nuts, preparing for winters
cold chill, making the mark you leave,
scratching out the cavern, carving the dunes,

moving great flocks of all types upon the lands, high in the sky, and deep in the ocean blue. The babies first gasp of air, the mothers collapse, the great effort so that life may continue. I am so in awe and inspired at every teardrop, the struggle, all parts of your journey teaching me that to love, give, and hold, is to allow. I see the suffering. I see the pain. I see the joy. I see the drive to win. I see it all. I see you. I want so much for you to come home. Every day I lookout. Every moment I think of you and honor all struggles. I hold no grudge. My hand is always outstretched. The gates are always open, a beacon lit with pure truth fed by the wellspring of eternal life. Calm still waters await. I will always, constantly, and forevermore tend the gate and host the welcoming warmly, wanting only to know of your story, your journey, your host, your king, your flickering beacon of hope and grace in the vast cold reaches of space. I will always be. All of the neglect sorrow and misery will be but a distant particle of continuation, forgotten, forgiven, another floating seed of creation continuing the expansive dance of life.

No more hurting. No more hiding.
No more fighting. No more shadows to hide
in. No more lies to be spewed. No more
misguided steps to follow. No more
switches for the controllers to control. No
more lost, wandering, shamed shattered
souls. No more spells to cast. No more
touching, taking, or taming. No more
pushing to the point of breaking. No more
scaffolding built upon the broken backs of
those less fortunate. No more ravenous
burning misogynistic desires. No more
blood stained, youth stolen underwear. No
more hidden moves or distractions. No
more treachery. No more celebration of
death. No more longing or pandering for the
ripest tender fruit on the vine. Nowhere to
run. Nowhere to hide. Nowhere to escape
the great hand as it sweeps into every crack,
crevice, and hidden hiding place as deaths
knock, your only fear, beats down your door
as the founders restore the sacred strands,
restoring the wellspring of eternal life.

In the face of total misery, Joy.
In the heart of destruction, Compassion.
In the home of malice, Contentedness.
In the closed hand of taking, Giving.
In the feet of the weary, Hope.
In the soul of those bitter, Forgiveness.
On the back of those carrying hatred, Love.
In the bones of rage, Patience.
In the arms of the downtrodden, Caring.
In the souls of those with nothing left to give
and no will to fight, Faith.